INTRODUCTION TO
THE WORK OF
BION

INTRODUCTION TO
THE WORK OF
BION

Groups, Knowledge, Psychosis, Thought,
Transformations, Psychoanalytic Practice

Leon Grinberg,
    Dario Sor and
        Elizabeth Tabak de Bianchedi

Translated from the Spanish by Alberto Hahn

JASON ARONSON, INC.
New York, N.Y.

Acknowledgments

The authors of this book have for the last eight years belonged to a study group, coordinated by one of us, devoted to the systematic study of Bion's work. The other members of the group who have collaborated with us in the production of this work are Drs. Julio A. Granel, Paulo Grimaldi, Ana G. de Kaplan, Silvio Lumermann, and Norberto Schlossberg. We wish now to record our gratitude and to warmly thank those colleagues for the discussion and elaboration of many ideas and the enriching comments which preceded the writing of this book.

We also remember with gratitude those who took part in the study group in the earlier days: Drs. A. Aizenberg, R. Avenburg, J. A. Carpinacci, L. A. Chiozza, G. S. de Foks, J. A. Olivares, H. Pastrana Borrero, R. Polito and E. Rolla.

Contents

Foreword

The man or woman looking at Vermeer's painting of the Little House in Delft may be aware of having an emotional experience such as he had not had before. Even I, reading this book, am aware that I had no idea what it might be like to be the reader of my books, or, at most a very imperfect idea. The psychoanalytic paradox is that the student hopes to learn in the course of his life and training what the human mind or personality is like; this would be useless if he did not learn, or was not by nature disposed to respect facts, and in this particular field the "fact" of the human personality. In this respect, then, he hopes to find that his patient is like all other human beings. The situation is complicated because he usually has to combine it with a respect for the uniqueness of the individual—as an individual, rather than as one of a crowd. How then is he to avoid on the one hand the danger of boredom and hostility and monotony of the common-place, and on the other the danger of taking a "particular" fact as a "generalization" of wide significance? It appears to be difficult to realize that the "discovery" (duly formulated or "interpreted" as we usually say) may have a "particular" significance, but no "general" importance. This in turn involves the capacity of the analyst to tolerate (respect) his own discoveries without having to believe they are of general significance or interest. I hope that this book will contribute to the achievement of this capacity.

W. R. Bion

Preface to the Second Edition

Since the first edition of this book, Bion has published several new contributions[1] rich in stimulating ideas and formulations. In one of these he points out that the analyst should tolerate the expanding universe appearing before him through his relationship with the patient. By the time an interpretation has been carried out, the universe has expanded beyond the analyst's own perception. Taking this model into consideration, we could add that since our *Introduction* first appeared the universe of concepts proposed by Bion has, thanks to his remarkable creative ability, continued to expand.

[1] "The Grid," Los Angeles, 1971 (unpublished); *Bion Brazilian Lectures 1—1973*, Imago Editora, Rio de Janeiro, 1973; *Bion Brazilian Lectures 2—1974*, Imago Editora, Rio de Janeiro, 1974; *A Memoir of the Future, Part I: The Dream*, Imago Editora, Rio de Janeiro, 1975.

We think, nonetheless, that the book retains its usefulness for readers interested in following the trail blazed by Bion: a trail leading into the enormous problems stemming from our investigation of the mind with the inadequate instruments at our disposal—in other words, the way toward the practice of psychoanalysis as opposed to "talking about psychoanalysis." We have therefore decided not to modify the form and structure of this essay in its second edition. We have merely added some footnotes related to the subsequent developments we have mentioned.

We insist on what we said in the Preface to the first edition: we hope this book will be not a substitute, but a mere prelude to the reading of the original texts by W. R. Bion.

Preface

We had many doubts before deciding to undertake what seemed a very risky and difficult venture: to write an introduction to Dr. Bion's ideas. On the one hand, we were encouraged by the requests of many colleagues and students who found great difficulty in comprehending the concepts he developed in his books; but at the same time we were held back by the responsibility of having to convey, in a simplified form, certain very complex hypotheses whose deep meaning has demanded from us long hours of work. An important encouragement in our decision to undertake this task was the great interest created by the courses, seminars, and study groups we held at different times; these allowed us to make better use of Bion's ideas. We will not describe all the vicissitudes of our task, but will mention only the particular impact of the experience of immersing ourselves in Bion's thought in all its depth and of finding it surprisingly coherent when we rediscovered, through his writings and early papers on group dynamics, the conducting thread of his original concepts. It was precisely this discovery that made us present the chapters in the order in which they appear.

One of Bion's greatest merits is that he had placed psychoanalytic theory and practice in a new dimension, preserving the most valuable classical contributions of Freud and Melanie Klein while approaching them from different perspectives (or "vertices."). He adds freshness and originality to them and stimulates a new attitude in the analyst by encouraging him to abandon rigid schemes and old clichés, thus opening up new ways of psychoanalytic thinking. The richness of his hypotheses, the scope of his theories, and the flexibility of his models, together with his advice of approaching the task of observation and investigation "without memory or desire," exercise an enormous attraction while at the same time provoking some uncertainty. All this tends to increase creative capacity, common sense, and the development of intuition, helping the investigator to get himself into what we would call "the state of discovery."

One of the obstacles in the understanding of the hypotheses proposed by Bion resides in his style of exposition, which is in a way a reflection of the hypotheses themselves. Bion speaks of the difficulties of expressing new ideas in familiar words; and this sometimes leads him to introduce terms that are intentionally devoid of meaning or to use familiar words in his own particular way. In our work of revision, synthesis, and transmission of his ideas we have tried to cope with this difficulty by introducing some of his concepts with greater specificity. It is possible that in achieving more clarity we may have lost some meaningful dimension of the ideas we are dealing with.

To provide a model of his theory of transformations, Bion uses at some point in his work the example of the reflection of a tree on the surface of a lake, where the observer can recognize the form but not the details of the structure. We believe that the emotional experience of reading Bion's papers is merely reflected in these pages. Many aspects and characteristics of the ideas described by us are reflections and do not show the original richness in all its details. In reading Bion one often feels that the depth and strength of his ideas is equivalent to agitating the surface of the lake and altering the reflection. Bion's language contains what appears as doubts, half-truths, mysteries, uncertainties; conveying these aspects of his ideas is in practice an impossible task.

We hope this book will awaken in the reader renewed curiosity and stimulate him to move on more boldly to the ineffable experience of reading Dr. Bion's ideas in the original.

INTRODUCTION TO
THE WORK OF
BION

GROUPS

In this chapter we shall deal with some of the hypotheses about groups that Bion formulated throughout his work. Therefore, we include ideas that appear in his papers about this subject, with special emphasis on certain points that will be developed later in this book. Such concepts as container-contained, catastrophic change, the mystic and the group etc., will be dealt with here only in relation to the main theme of this chapter: the groups and their dynamics.

The Individual and the Group

The human being is a gregarious animal. He cannot avoid being a member of a group, even when belonging to a group consists in behaving in such a way as to give the impression of not belonging to any group. Group experiences allow us to observe the "political" characteristics of the human being, not because these are created by the group but because it is necessary to have a group gathering for them to become manifest and thus become the object of observation. Excessive importance has been attributed to the gathering of the group because of the erroneous impression that something necessarily starts at the moment its existence becomes demonstrable.

Bion suggests that no individual, even in isolation, can be considered marginal to a group or lacking the active manifestations of group psychology, even when the conditions to demonstrate this are not present.

Freud's theories, and among them the Oedipus complex,[1] show us the enormous importance of the family group in the development of the human being. Melanie Klein's work, particularly her hypotheses about early object relations, psychotic anxieties, and primitive defense mechanisms,[2] allows us to understand not only that the individual belongs to a family group from the beginning of his life, but also that his first contacts with his mother and other persons of his surroundings have a quality that is in itself peculiar and of profound importance for his ultimate development. The psychotic anxieties aroused in relation to the first objects are reactivated in various adult situations. The individual must establish contact with the emotional life of the group, which poses the dilemma of evolution and differentiation, and of having to face the fears associated with this evolution. The demands and complexities derived from belonging to various groups lead him to a regression that can be related to that described by M. Klein in the context of psychoanalytic theory.

The *observation* of groups by a psychoanalytically trained observer allows the detection of situations that from another perspective could be overlooked. *Psychoanalytic theories,* and among them the Oedipus complex and the Kleinian theories[3] of psychotic anxieties and early defense mechanisms, can be used to explain some of the observed phenomena. Psychoanalytically developed intuition allows us to make observations in which the emotional reactions of the observer, included in the situation, are taken into account in the description, understanding, and interpretation of the phenomena.

This is how Bion approaches the study of groups.

One of his first experiences with groups as objects of study took place while he was the Director of the rehabilitation center of a military psychiatric hospital during the Second World War. The patients had to be trained to be able to return to the military task, and Bion proposed that rehabilitation should be considered a group problem, organizing the Section in his charge—composed of many hundreds of men—according to this plan. This project was developed for six weeks and consisted of a program that required all men to have one hour a day of physical training and to be members of one or more groups where they could study handicrafts. According to the different interests that emerged, the individuals could form groups for the development of these interests. Daily meetings were held with all the patients, staff, and directors to discuss the programs, the new problems that were created, and the decisions to be taken. This item in the program was the first step toward the organization of therapeutic seminars.

The results of this experience, in which some characteristics of the groups in relation to the planned tasks became clear, showed the need for a more careful examination of the structure and dynamic interaction within the group. Later on, at the Tavistock Clinic in London, Bion worked as a therapist with small groups of patients. With the specific purpose of helping to clarify the tensions that appeared in these groups and with a technique that consisted of a description of the situations within the group that appeared to oppose the proposed task, he elaborated some hypotheses about the complex group phenomena he was observing.

The facts that first attracted his attention in work with different groups were related to the behavior of the individuals in the group context and emotional climate that developed in that situation. The groups that congregated to carry out a specific task showed attitudes and developed methods that did not seem conducive to the achievement of the proposed aim. These were manifest in the absence of intellectual richness in the conversations during the sessions; in the diminution of critical judgment; and in disturbances in the rational behavior of its members which did not in general link up with their ability and intelligence outside the group situation. Solutions to problems within the group were not found by using methods in tune with reality.

The situations created in the group were intensely charged with emotions. These emotions exercised a powerful influence on its members and seemed to orientate the group activity, without the members perceiving that this was happening. The therapist shared in this intense and often chaotic emotional climate, to which all the members contribute to some extent. The group did not appear prepared to examine these situations.

The group frequently seemed to function as a unit or whole, even though this unit did not become manifest in the individual contributions. This mode of functioning became more evident when the group was considered from a different perspective; observing the group as a whole, rather than its members, allowed certain facts to acquire new meaning.

In his active participation in various groups as an adult, the human being has different ways of reacting. When a number of people meet to carry out a task one may find two tendencies: one directed toward the accomplishment of the task and another that seems to oppose it. Work is obstructed by a more regressive and primary activity. Referring to these phenomena, which he considers typical, Bion introduces a specific terminology that gives a certain unity to the common features observed in different experiences. These terms are: group mentality–group culture, basic assumptions, basic-assumption groups, and work group.

Group Mentality-Group Culture

The hypothesis of the existence of a *group mentality* derives from the fact that the group often functions as a unit, even though its members may not intend this, nor be aware of it.

The term then defines the collective mental activity that takes place when people get together in a group. It also delineates an area of investigation in which one can make observations and draw hypotheses. As a term, it represents a "constant conjunction"[4] that will acquire further meaning as the investigation proceeds. The hypothesis of a group mentality is the basic formulation to investigate group phenomena.

Group mentality is formed by the unanimous opinion, willpower, or desire of the group at a certain moment. The members contribute to it anonymously and unconsciously. Group mentality can be in conflict with the desires, opinions, and thoughts of the individuals and can produce in them uneasiness, anger, or other reactions.

The group organization may, at a certain moment, be seen as the result of the interplay between group mentality and the desires of the individuals. This organization, primitive and rudimentary though it may be, is called by Bion *group culture*. This concept comprises the structure acquired by the group at a given moment, the task it proposes to carry out, and the organization it adopts for this purpose. The group culture is a fact that can be observed within the context of the group situation, and that can be described by the observer through taking into account the behavior of its members, the roles they perform, the acting leaders, and the behavior of the group as a whole.

Group culture is a function[5] of the group mentality and of the desires of the individual, which are its factors. The organization the group adopts at a given moment, or during a certain period of time, stems from the conflict between the anonymous and unconscious collective willpower and the individual's wishes and needs.

To give greater precision to the concept of group mentality, Bion introduces the term *basic assumption*.

Basic Assumptions

Basic assumption is a term qualifying the concept of group mentality. It will be remembered that this concept refers to the existence of a common, unanimous, and anonymous opinion at a given moment. Group mentality is the recipient or *container* of all the contributions made by the members of the group. The concept of basic assumption tells us something about the content, or possible different contents, of this opinion, allowing a greater understanding of the emotional phenomena in the groups.

Basic assumptions are shaped by the intense emotions of primitive origin, and are for this reason considered basic. Their existence partly determines the organization the group will adopt and the way in which it will approach the task it is to carry out. Therefore, the group culture will always show evidence of the underlying group assumptions or the specific basic assumption active at any moment.

In the group, the underlying emotional impulses, the basic assumptions, express a shared fantasy of an omnipotent or magic type as to how to achieve its goals and satisfy its desires. These impulses, characterized by their irrational content, have a strength and reality manifest in group behavior. It is important to point out that the basic assumptions are unconscious and often opposed to the conscious rational opinions of the members of the group.

The term *group in a certain basic assumption* refers to the specific structure and organization adopted by the group in reference to the active basic assumption. Opposed to this organization is the one based on the *work group*, a concept dealt with later on. The basic assumptions described by Bion are three. The first is called *basic assumption of independence* (baD) and can be reformulated in narrative terms as follows: the group holds the conviction that it is meeting so that somebody on whom the group depends absolutely should satisfy all its needs and desires. We could say that the collective belief is that there is an external object whose function is to provide security for the group as an "immature organism." In other words credence is given to a protective deity whose goodness, potency, and wisdom are not questioned. The *basic assumption of fight-flight* (baF) consists in the group's conviction that there is an enemy who must be attacked or avoided. In other words, the bad object is external and the only defensive activity vis à vis this object is its destruction (fight) or avoidance (flight).

The *basic assumption of pairing* (baP) is, in narrative terms, the collective and unconscious belief that, whatever the present problems and needs of the group, something in the future or somebody still unborn will solve it: in other words that there exists a messianic hope. This irrational and primitive hope is essential for the basic assumption of pairing. Hope is often put in a couple whose unborn child will be the savior. In this emotional state what matters is the idea of the future, rather than the solution of present problems. In religious terms it is the hope of the birth of the messiah.

To sum up, we may say that basic assumptions are the equivalent for the group of omnipotent fantasies about the way its difficulties will be resolved. The techniques that are used are magical. All basic assumptions are emotional states that tend to *avoid* the frustration implied in learning from experience, when learning implies effort, pain, and contact with reality.

The conceptualization of the three basic assumptions allows some order to emerge from often obscure emotional situations in the groups. By defining three broad emotional configurations, Bion has given the observer a new instrument for the understanding of the phenomena he participates in. The similarity of the characteristics of the basic assumptions to the phenomena described by Melanie Klein in her theories about part objects, psychotic anxieties, and primitive defenses[6] allows us to assume that the basic assumption phenomena are the group reactions to psychotic anxieties reactivated by the individual's dilemma in the group and the regression this dilemma imposes on him.

Basic Assumption Group

How does a group with a specific predominant basic assumption function? In each case it is necessary to analyze the structures that develop, taking into account the active basic assumption and the individual needs and opinions of the members of the group, whether these do or do not coincide with the basic assumption.

The individuals who take part in the activity called basic assumption do so in an automatic and inevitable way, without needing any special training, emotional experience, or mental maturity. Participation in this does not require from group members a capacity to cooperate, which is a fundamental requisite for taking part in the mental activity that is called work group. To differentiate spontaneous participation in a basic assumption group from the conscious or unconscious participation in the work group, Bion proposes to use the word *cooperation* for the latter and *valency* for the instinctive capacity to participate in the mental and group activity according to basic assumptions. Valency, a term taken from physics, indicates the individual's greater or lesser readiness to enter into basic assumption activity. With this analogy Bion qualifies his opinion that this capacity, even though it arises in or can be deduced from psychological phenomena, characterizes a level of behavior more analogous to plant tropism than to purposive behavior. The group therapist also participates in this level of functioning and faces in the group the same (or at least a similar) dilemma to that of the other members.

The basic assumption groups or *basic groups,* as Bion also calls them, have certain typical forms of organization, especially when it comes to leadership and behavior. The descriptions that follow are taken mostly from situations in small therapeutic groups led with Bion's technique. The concepts are nevertheless applicable to the understanding of such large human groups as the army, religious communities, and social classes.

The culture called *dependent group,* founded on that particular basic assumption organizes itself to seek a leader who can fulfill its needs. This role of leader is easily assigned to the coordinating therapist, and one can often see that the idea of "receiving treatment" expresses an expectation that goes much further than is rational or logical.

The dependent group behaves vis à vis the therapist as if it were convinced that all the work has to be carried out by him. Loss of critical judgment and passivity, for instance, are evidence of this configuration. The group can organize itself like pupils before a professor from whom it expects to receive instructions or from whom it can demand such provision. It can also function as a group of disciples of an idea or a person whose goodness is not questioned, or as a group of children waiting to be treated individually and in turn.

When the therapist interprets, committed as he is to the emotional situation in the group, he will perceive an uneasiness derived from frustration of the group's expectations. If, by pointing out group fantasies, he denies his role of provider or suggests the need to clarify the underlying situations—an activity that conveys to the group his refusal

to assume the role assigned to him and his request that the
members should function at a more adult level—the group
may react (in a different way) to impending danger. A
possible outcome is that, while maintaining its basic
assumption, it will look for another person or idea to
become the deified leader. Sometimes it is the most ill
member of the group who replaces the therapist as leader. At
other times leadership is referred back to the group history,
the group "bible," and much time is spent in producing this
and teaching from it. This activity consists of remembering
or appealing to the traditions of the group and acts as a
"memory" that opposes the evolution of new ideas.

Another vicissitude is the substitution of a different basic
assumption, with a corresponding change in emotional
climate, leadership, and roles. In extreme cases of conflict
with the new idea (in our example, the idea proposed by the
therapist with his interpretation of the group mentality), the
group may react by producing a new form of organization
that needs the participation of an extraneous group. This
form of reacting is called *aberrant form* and consists, in the
case of the dependent group, of an attempt to put pressure
through action on some external group to make it exercise
its influence, or to be influenced by it.

Because of his own valency, the group therapist is always
exposed to the danger of functioning at the level of basic
assumption. This is shown by changes in his attitude or
alterations in his technique—for example, by giving
interpretation to the individual within the group instead of
focusing on the group as a whole. By this behavior he helps
to give shape to the collective belief that he is a kind of deity
reinforcing the role that is attributed to him. These and
other emotional responses can be seen as phenomena related
to difficulty in maintaining a scientific level of work in a
disturbed field, as is the basic assumption group. The culture
called *basic assumption of fight-flight* finds its leader in
paranoid personalities. The leader must support the idea

that there is an enemy inside or outside the group from whom it is necessary to defend itself or escape. In the therapeutic group the enemy can be a member of the group, the therapist himself, his words, physical or mental illness, etc. The group may adopt an organization whose main aim is to avoid any manifestion of the "enemy," or to shift it into some subgroup which is therefore attacked. When the therapist is considered the enemy, the group will ignore his intervention or show its contempt through words or action. Hostility, like dependency, may assume different forms. The aberrant forms of this type of culture is expressed in activities that tend to take possession of the person of the therapist or of external groups, or to be possessed by external groups, their ideas or opinions.

In the culture called *pairing group,* leadership is related to a couple who promise to produce a child, or some idea related to the future; the leader is something or somebody as yet unborn. Pairing can be established between two members in a dialogue; the rest of the group not only tolerate but also stimulate this relationship. It does not react with jealousy or rivalry because this couple is considered to contain the hope of the birth of the future leader who will save the group. This is the messianic hope that an idea or a person will save it from its feelings of hatred, destructiveness, or despair. Clearly, for this to happen a messianic hope must never be fulfilled. In the culture dominated by this basic assumption, the therapist with his highly stimulated curiosity may also participate in the messianic hope with the subsequent loss of his efficiency as an observer. The aberrant form of this type of group is the tendency to schism.

When facing the threat of the evolution of a new idea (what Bion calls in another context a messianic idea, to be differentiated from the messianic hope), the group can split defensively. Once the schism is produced, a part of the group will continue holding the messianic hope, i.e. will continue under the basic assumption of pairing. The vicissitudes of the other part will depend on a new series of factors, foremost among them tolerance to the new idea and its tendency to function again as a basic assumption group.

It is important to point out that the aberrant form of culture appears only when the group has to face a new idea that promotes evolution and that it cannot take place in a work group culture nor neutralize a basic assumption culture. The evolution of the new idea threatens the basic group structure, and brings with it the possibility of a situation that Bion calls *catastrophic change*.

Basic assumptions can alternate within the same session or remain the same for many months, but they never coexist. The emotions associated with them can be described in common terms of anxiety, fear, love, sex, hate, etc.; nevertheless, anxiety in a dependent group has a different quality from anxiety in a fight-flight or a pairing group, and similarly with other emotions.

According to these descriptions it seems clear that the methods with which the group functions under a certain assumption are primitive and unrealistic. The tenacity with which the basic group adheres to these primitive methods is due to the intensity of the feelings and to the mechanisms of projective identification it uses to defend itself from psychotic anxieties.

One characteristic common to all basic assumption groups is the hostility with which they oppose any stimulus for growth or development. In the therapeutic group the stimulus toward growth and development is directly related to *insight;* the basic assumption group fiercely opposes this possibility.

Another characteristic refers to the use of language. In the basic group, language is not developed as a method of thought, but is used as a form of action. One could say that it is language stripped of its communicative quality, a quality that depends on the formation and utilization of symbols. Language in a basic group is in this respect more similar to the language of the psychotic than to that of the neurotic. The basic assumption group does not include the notion of time and therefore does not tolerate frustration. This situation is very closely related to the incapacity to develop symbolic language that could be used as a prelude to action, the *language of achievement,* as Bion calls it.

Work Group

When speaking of basic assumptions we referred mainly to the primitive emotional level that manifests itself in every group. It is important to understand that this primitive level always coexists with another level of functioning that is the one belonging to the work group.

Work group is a term used by Bion to refer to a particular type of group mentality and to a culture that derives from it. The work group (W) requires from its members cooperation and effort; it is not a function of valency but results from a certain maturity and training for participating in it. It is a mental state that implies contact with reality, tolerance of frustrations, and control of emotions, and is similar in its characteristics to the ego as a psychic entity, as described by Freud.[7] The organization of the group (the group culture) as a function of group mentality in the work group is different from the organization (the group culture) that appears in the basic assumption. At this level of functioning of the work group, the task to be carried out by the group implies the use of rational and scientific methods of approach. The leader is the person who is most efficient in providing the possibility of such an approach. The task, which can be painful, promotes the growth and maturity in the group and its members. In a therapeutic group the therapist is the leader of this function

Verbal exchange is a function of the work group, as is the action that results from it. The work group that tolerates frustration allows the evolution of new ideas and these will not be deified, denied, or evacuated; their progress will not be obstructed, as happens in the basic assumption group. The coexistence of the basic assumption group and of the work group brings about a permanent conflict that always recurs within the group. The activity of the work group is disrupted by the basic assumption group; the tendency the individual has to differentiate himself is opposed by his regressive tendency not to do so. The conflict can be formulated in different ways: as a conflict between a new idea and the group, or between the work group and the basic assumption. The basic assumption group is opposed to the new idea, as described in our previous formulation of this theme. The work group and the individual within the group face the pain of opposing both tendencies. The individual as a person in the work group is exposed to the inevitable component of loneliness, isolation, and pain associated with growth and evolution. (See Appendix § 1.)

The Specialized Work Group

Society as a group also shows basic phenomena. In their growth, social groups have partly resolved this problem by delegating, as it were, some containing functions to certain subgroups. Bion calls these organizations and institutions the *specialized work groups*.

Applying these hypotheses it is possible to consider such institutions as the church or army as subgroups which fulfill the function of specialized work groups for the rest of society. From this point of view, the church with its organization and structure embodies the basic assumption of dependence; the army embodies the basic assumption of fight-flight, freeing the rest of society from the task of having to contain these basic assumptions. There are groups specialized in the basic assumption of pairing; the aristocracy as a social class, with its ideas on race and birth, is one example.

Failure to contain efficiently the relevant basic assumption in one of these institutionalized subgroups—because it is particularly active, or because for some reason it is replaced by another—will provoke reactions in the subgroup or in the society of which it is part. One may then find a new and different structure evolving, or the reactivation of a tendency to avoid it. The concept of specialized work group provides a new perspective for understanding the complex phenomena of society in general.

Catastrophic Change

Catastrophic change is a term chosen by Bion to describe the constant conjunction of facts that can be found in diverse fields, among them the mind, the group, the psychoanalytic session, and society. The facts referred to by the constant conjunction can be observed when a new idea appears in any of the areas mentioned.

Bion states that the new idea contains a potentially disruptive force, which violates to a greater or lesser degree the structure of the field in which it appears. Thus a new discovery violates the structure of the preexisting theory, a revolutionary the structure of society, an interpretation the structure of the personality. Referring in particular to the facts as they occur in small therapeutic groups, the new idea expressed in an interpretation or represented in the person of a new member promotes a change in the group structure. One structure is transformed into another through stages of disorganization, pain, and frustration; growth will be a function of these vicissitudes. Using the model of container and contained it is possible to study these vicissitudes without referring to the particular field in which they take place. It is possible to refer to the new idea as the *contained,* and the group, the mind, or society as a *container,* and study their possible interactions (see chapter 3).

We are now in a condition to specify the facts that Bion links to the term *catastrophic change.* These are *violence, invariance,* and *subversion of the system;* he considers these elements inherent in any situation of growth. The term *invariance* refers to that which allows recognition in a new structure of aspects of the old one (see chapter 4).

The vicissitudes of the new idea (contained within the group container) have been referred to partly by describing the evasive tendencies of the basic assumption group when faced with anything that implies evolution. Attempts to evacuate, deify, or dogmatize are defensive reactions in the face of catastrophic change. We can apply this model to any scientific, religious, therapeutic, or social group. Freud, for example, gave birth to a new and revolutionary idea; some groups rejected and expelled his ideas, and other groups organized themselves around him, forming institutions which performed the function of containing and transforming his ideas. In a very different context, Christ and his ideas provoked defensive and schismatic reactions in groups where one can find the same underlying configuration.

The Mystic and the Group

The exceptional individual can be described in different ways. One can call him a genius, a mystic, or a messiah. Bion prefers to use the term *mystic* to refer to exceptional individuals in any field, whether scientific, artistic, or religious. He uses the word *Establishment,* a term currently in fashion to designate those who exercise power and responsibility in the state or in other institutions, to refer to whatever exercises these functions in the personality or in the group.

The mystic or genius, bearer of a new idea, is always disruptive for the group; the Establishment tries to protect the group from this disruption. The problem that arises from the relation between the mystic-genius and the institution creates an emotional configuration that repeats itself in different forms throughout history. The mystic needs the Establishment and vice versa; the institutionalized group (work group) is as important to the development of the individual as is the individual to the work group.

The mystic-genius may present himself to the group as a revolutionary or may maintain, on the contrary, that he is in complete agreement with the regulations that govern the group. He can be creative or nihilistic and will certainly be considered both—at some point—by different parts of the group. It is a fact that every genius, mystic, or messiah is both things, as the nature of his contributions is bound to destroy certain laws or conventions, the culture or coherence of some group, or of some subgroup within a group. The disruptive power of the mystic-genius is limited by the means by which he transmits his message, and his creative qualities as a promoter of change will depend on his language of achievement. The Establishment must achieve, as one of its functions, an appropriate containment and representation of the new creative idea, partly limiting its disruptive power and at the same time making it accessible to all the members of the group who are not geniuses. The reader can find many examples of these configurations in fields as varied as that of history of religions, the discovery of psychoanalysis, and the discoveries of science and their institutionalization.

The relation between the mystic-genius and the group may belong to one of three categories. It can be *commensal, symbiotic* or *parasitic*. In the commensal relationship the mystic-genius and the group coexist without affecting each other; there is no confrontation or change even though there might be some change if the relation changes. In the symbiotic relationship a confrontation takes place that will eventually be benefical to both; the ideas of the mystic-genius are analyzed and taken into account, and his contributions generate benevolence or hostility. This relationship produces as much growth in the mystic-genius as it does in the group, even though this growth is not easily detectable. The predominant emotions are love, hate, and knowledge (see chapter 6). In the parasitic relationship, where envy is the main factor, the product of the association is the destruction and stripping of both the mystic-genius and the group. An example among the many possible is a group which promotes an individual who is exceptional in his creative-destructive role to a position in the Establishment where his energies are absorbed by administrative functions.

The recurrent configuration in these descriptions is one of an explosive force within a framework which tries to contain it. In the case of the group, this configuration takes place between the mystic-genius and the Establishment with its function of containing, expressing, and institutionalizing the new idea provided by him and of protecting the group from the destructive power of this idea.

Notes

1. S. Freud, The Ego and the id, S.E. 19.
2. M. Klein, "Some theoretical conclusions regarding the emotional life of the infant," in *Developments in Psychoanalysis*, Hillary House, New York, 1952.
3. Ibid.
4. *Constant conjunction* is a term taken from Hume and refers to the fact that certain observed data regularly appear together. Bion uses this term in his hypothesis about the development of thought. A concept of a word are definitions that bind the observed elements that are constantly conjoined.

5. The term *function* is used by Bion in the mathematical, philosophical, and ordinary language sense, with the explicit aim of keeping the associations derived from these areas from being limited by previous penumbrae of meaning.

6. M. Klein, op. cit.

7. S. Freud, op. cit.

Chapter 2

PSYCHOSIS

The Individual and Psychosis • Psychotic Personality •
Thought and Language in Individuals with a Predominantly Psychotic Personality • Clinical Transference
Manifestations of the Psychotic Personality • Catastrophic Change in the Psychotic Crisis

In this chapter, we describe some concepts of psychosis, its clinical manifestations, and the hypotheses about its origin and development. In the understanding of phenomena associated with the psychotic process, Bion regards it as fundamentally important to conceptualize the *psychotic personality* as exemplifying a mental state with characteristics predominantly manifest in seriously disturbed patients.

The papers published by Bion on themes related to psychosis follow chronologically his work on groups. Some of these papers are predominantly clinical and include clinical material. Others are more theoretical and develop hypotheses about thought and language in the schizophrenic. These papers (1950–1962) were then brought together by Bion in his *Second Thoughts*[1] and are analyzed as a whole and in detail in the commentary at the end of the volume.

The patients whose material are used in the formulation of some of the hypotheses described in this chapter were treated by Bion in a psychoanalytic setting which did not differ from the one usually employed for neurotic patients, even though in some cases the patients were diagnosed as schizophrenics. The technique used was always exclusively interpretive, taking into account the positive and the negative transference and applying Kleinian concepts for the understanding of the material: such concepts as part-object relations, the paranoid-schizoid and depressive positions, and the theories of envy, of primitive defense mechanisms, and, in particular, of splitting and projective identification.

The Individual and Psychosis

The individual, whatever his stage of development, faces emotional phenomena of different kinds and resolves them in a particular way. For this task he uses his consciousness, which, analogous to the sense organs, is considered by Freud "a sense organ for the perception of psychical qualities."[2] Bion postulates its existence in a rudimentary form from the beginning of life. Its development requires stimuli that at first consist of feelings and later on of the whole range of mental phenomena. Contact with internal and external reality is very closely linked to this "organ" and the way of approaching such reality depends on its way of functioning. The multiple experiences of the individual in his contact with himself and with others imply an unavoidable confrontation between his tendency to "have consciousness" and not to have it, between his tendency to tolerate it and to avoid it. This confrontation and its consequences give rise to different configurations in different individual mentalities, one of which is the *psychotic personality,* or psychotic part of the personality.

In this context, the psychotic personality is not a psychiatric diagnosis but designates a way of mental functioning that coexists with other ways of functioning. According to the dominance of one way of functioning over another, certain behavior will become observable and thus determine a diagnosis of psychosis or neurosis in the clinical sense. For the psychoanalyst the psychiatric diagnosis has a relative value; this diagnosis is important for those people who deal with hospital admissions and physical care of patients: psychiatrists, nurses, specialized staff. The psychoanalytic point of view is different, especially when it assumes, as Bion does, that all individuals, even the most developed, potentially contain mental functions and responses derived from the psychotic personality, manifesting themselves as hostility toward the mental apparatus, consciousness, and internal and external reality. The main objective of the analyst is to understand and interpret such phenomena when they become observable.

The Psychotic Personality

The concept of psychotic personality refers, then, rather to a mental state than to a psychiatric diagnosis; the term defines a form of mental functioning that is manifest in behavior, in language, and in the effect it has on the observer. Bion considers that this mental state always coexists with another mental state that is conceptualized as the *non-psychotic personality;* the individual in analysis will show evidence of both, with a dominance of one or the other and with different degrees of organization and stability.

It is possible to approach the investigation of the psychotic personality from different angles: through its manifestations in behavior or language, or from certain genetic hypotheses that study its origin, structure, and activity. It is important to differentiate the mental mechanisms that form part of its organization and structure, and to correlate these mechanisms with those used by the non-psychotic personality or neurotic part of the personality.

One of the outstanding features of the psychotic personality is the intolerance to frustration which, together with a predominance of destructive impulses, manifests itself as violent hatred of internal and external reality. This hatred also extends to the senses and the parts of the personality and psychic elements that are used to establish contact with this reality and its recognition, to consciousness and all the functions associated with it.[3] Because of the intensity of the destructive impulses, love is transformed into sadism and the conflict between the life and death instincts is not resolved. The psychotic personality is also characterized by the fear of imminent annihilation, which contributes to the specific type of object relations that are established, among them the analytic transference; these are premature and hasty relationships that settle in tenaciously and are extremely precarious and fragile.

The attack directed against aspects of the self results in the main mental activities, especially the perceptual apparatus as well as the link with objects, appearing mutilated and transformed into small particles that are violently expelled. These evacuated particles can be experienced as having an independent and uncontrolled life that threatens dangerously from outside. The evacuation of these particles takes place through pathological projective identification.

The mechanism of projective identification was described by M. Klein[4] and was included in her hypotheses on the emotional development of the first months of life. Projective identification consists in the omnipotent fantasy that the unwanted parts of the personality and internal objects can be disowned, projected, and controlled in the object into which they have been projected. This mechanism, which is part of the primitive defenses used in the first months of life, acquires a different modality of functioning during the transition from the paranoid-schizoid position to the depressive position. The normal functioning of projective identification constitutes one of the main factors in symbol formation and human communication, and determines a relationship of empathy with the object by providing the possibility of putting oneself in somebody else's place and, in doing so, to understand his feelings better.

The mechanism of projective identification is character-ized as follows: parts of the ego are projected into the object, causing this object to be experienced as controlled by the projected parts and imbued with their qualities. This mechanism, active from the beginning of life, may have various functions: of relieving the ego of bad parts; of preserving good parts by protecting them from a bad internal world; of attacking and destroying the object; etc. One of the consequences of this process is that, by projecting the bad parts (including fantasies and bad feelings) into a good breast (an understanding object), the infant will be able—insofar as his development allows—to reintroject the same parts in a more tolerable form, once they have been modified by the thought (reverie) of the object.

Bion attaches great importance to this mechanism and considers it the origin of an activity that will later be described as the capacity to think (see chapter 3). On the other hand, he describes a form of *pathological projective identification,* which takes place in certain psychotic illnesses or which is used by the psychotic personality where there is a predominance of envy and greed. In this case, the splitting of parts of the ego is so severe that it results in a multiplicity of minute fragments which are violently projected into the object. These fragments, which are expelled by pathological projective identification, create a reality populated by *bizarre objects* and which becomes increasingly painful and persecuting. The consequence of this is a further increase of projective identification. This pathological splitting and projection increasingly damages the perceptual and judging apparatus, and results in further withdrawal from reality.

The term *bizarre object* was created by Bion to describe

the kind of objects by which the psychotic patient feels surrounded. Through pathological splitting and projective identification, he tries to rid himself not only of the object, but also and deliberately of all the ego functions connected with the incipient reality principle (primitive thoughts, consciousness, attention, judgment), especially of those elements that have a linking function. In the patient's belief, the particles of ego function that are fragmented and violently evacuated penetrate and occupy the real objects and engulf them. In turn, the engulfed object attacks the projected part of the personality and strips it of vitality. This results in a bizarre object, composed of a part of the personality and parts of the object, in a relation of container-contained (♀ ♂) that strips both of vitality and meaning. The particle of personality has been transformed into a "thing."

In terms of the theory of development of thought, the bizarre object is formed by beta elements, residues of the ego, of the superego, and of external objects. The bizarre objects are primitive and complex and have a very unstable nature, as they depend on the fragmented and projected aspects of the ego and superego that invade the real object. The psychotic patient's attempt to use these elements for thinking makes him take primitive thoughts for real objects and makes him deal with the latter according to the laws of mental functioning; but when he discovers that these real objects obey the laws of natural science he feels confused. The psychotic part of the personality places in the real world what the non-psychotic person represses: his unconscious seems to have been replaced by a world of bizarre objects. Bion points out that the psychotic patient moves, "not in a world of dreams" but in a world of bizarre objects that are similar to what corresponds in the non-psychotic personality to the "furniture of dreams." He feel locked up in this world, as he must use these bizarre objects instead of using what for the non-psychotic personality would be thoughts.

He is incapable of escaping because he feels he lacks an apparatus of consciousness that is the key to getting out and freeing himself from this captivity. This description allows us to understand that the psychotic personality does not have the essential instruments for the development of verbal thought.

Bion abstracted the model of the relationship "container-contained" from a particular aspect of projective identification, which afforded further insight into this mechanism. According to this model, the infant projects a part of his psyche, especially his uncontrollable emotions (the contained), into the good breast-container, only to receive them back "detoxified" and in a more tolerable form. He used the signs ♀ , ♂ to represent the container and the contained respectively; these signs simultaneously designate and represent.

The container-contained model is applicable to many situations, as will be seen when we study the different themes developed in this book. But what we want to point out now is the *use* of the model as being one of the main features of projective identification that represents the dynamic relationship of "container-contained." This relationship can be developmental or non-developmental according to the quality of the emotion which impregnates it. If, for example, it is impregnated by envy, the elements container-contained are stripped of their essential qualities (meaning, vitality) and produce a model that is the antithesis of the model used for growth. Bion uses the minus sign, – ♀ ♂ , to represent what has just been described. The psychoanalytic relationship provides emotional experiences that approximate to this description.

In contrast, when ♀ ♂ represents a growing relationship, it is represented by + ♀ ♂ . The main difference from – ♀ ♂ is that + ♀ ♂ has the possibility of a development, based on tolerance of doubt and on a sense of the infinite. Instead, – ♀ ♂ does not develop; on the contrary, it permanently suffers spoiling attacks that populate the mental space with bizarre objects: things—in themselves. When the psychotic part of the personality is dominated by – ♀ ♂ it tends to organize a "Super" ego that is in omniscient opposition to learning from experience. This "Super" ego, as Bion calls it, is opposed to scientific development and is guided by moral principles that disregard reality-based notions of good and evil. It emerges from the confusing consequences of excessive pathological projective identification, and its "moral" criteria could be defined as an affirmation of destructive superiority, a determination to possess in order to stop what is possessed from having an existence of its own.

The superego, as it is normally understood, has the power of provoking guilt feelings. "Super" ego, as described by Bion, retains this power, but its characteristic is that the guilt to which it gives rise is extremely persecutory.[5] The psychotic personality uses this power, as can be seen in clinical experience with severely disturbed patients.

To sum up: the main factor differentiating the psychotic from the non-psychotic parts of the personality (if it is at all possible to isolate such a factor), is the sadistic attack on the ego and on the matrix of thinking and on the projective identification into the fragments that takes place at the beginning of the patient's life. From this point onward the psychotic personality differs more and more from the non-psychotic; the former does not develop and the latter does. In the psychotic personality, the attack is repeated and becomes more complex; there is no synthesis but agglomeration; projective identification and splitting are used as substitutes for repression; envious and cruel feelings make the incorporation of objects (in this case of bizarre objects) seem a "projective identification in reverse"—that is, the objects return via the same route by which they were expelled and with the same or even greater hostility. The psychotic personality can be represented as a destructive mental state, as a violent force that, like an object, can be described as greedy, envious, cruel, and murderous. The existence of this force is determined by an innate disposition; its development is related to that of the first object relations.

To understand how the psychotic personality arises and develops we must consider a congenital disposition, as well as the relationship with a mother who was unable to perform her function of receiving, containing, and modifying the violent emotions projected by the child. (See Appendix § 2.)

Thought and Language in Individuals with a Predominantly Psychotic Personality

Bion assumes that the disorders of thought so obvious in the psychotic and sometimes discernible in apparently better integrated personalities are based on intolerance to frustration and on the persistence of the mechanism of pathological projective identification as just described. An important aspect of the pathological functioning of the mechanism used by the psychotic personality is determined by this incapacity to tolerate frustration. It tries to *avoid* frustration, producing beta elements (see chapter 3) which cannot be differentiated from the "thing in itself," instead of trying to *modify* frustration by producing alpha elements which would lead to a *representation* of the "thing in itself" (see chapter 3). In such cases, there will be a disturbance in the development of the apparatus to think thoughts, with a hypertrophic increase of projective identification resulting in a permanent evacuation of whatever is related to frustration, pain, and awareness of that situation. The evasion of frustration and pain can be achieved by destructively attacking the part of the mental apparatus that is able to perceive them. The limits between the self and the external object are blurred and the functions of communication are contaminated by the tendency to evacuate. If intolerance to frustration is not so great as to use the mechanisms of evasion but strong enough to predominate over the reality principle, the personality will develop with omnipotence and omniscience as a substitute for the learning process and there will not be a function of psychic activity that can discriminate between the true and false; there will also be an absence of thought capable of genuine symbolization.

Patients with serious learning problems who try to solve them by using their aptitude for imitation try to reproduce ·with mimicry all that the object does, shows, or teaches. In fact, imitation is a valuable capacity, a stage in the evolution of learning for the normal child. But in psychotic children (with envy and marked intolerance to frustration) this imitation substitutes for learning based on understanding, assimilation, and manipulation of symbols. They cannot use normal projective identification for the purpose of learning; in projecting they confuse and lose all notion of differentiation between self and object. Instead they use pathological projective identification and imitation. Bion mentions a dramatic clinical example of a schizophrenic adolescent patient that illustrates many of the problems of the psychotic personality. This adolescent had murdered his parents and had thrown their corpses down a cliff to free himself concretely from the internal parental couple and his feelings of hatred toward them that, according to him, made it impossible to have a loving sexual relationship with his girlfriend. He was then condemned because in his trial he stated that he "knew" he had done something "bad," as through imitation he was repeating what other people said about the crime. In fact, he could not discriminate between "goodness" and "badness" and had therefore no capacity for discernment; nor was he responsible for his acts.

The particles evacuated as a consequence of splitting and of pathological projective identification contain—as we have mentioned—parts of the ego, parts of objects, and parts of the perceptual apparatus linked to form the bizarre objects mentioned earlier on. These particles have to be put again under control so that the psychotic personality can attempt to develop a verbal language. The patient depends on these particles—used as prototypes of ideas—to form the matrix from which words will emerge. His confusion will increase when he has to use these bizarre objects to form his thoughts. From what is left of the psychotic disaster, he will attempt to reconstruct his language. As, on the other hand, these patients are apt to be hyperdestructive, they attack the links of the incipient thoughts of the non-psychotic part of the personality as well as the links of sense impressions together with their consciousness. As a result of this the objects can never come into contact in such a way that their intrinsic qualities remain intact and able to combine to produce a new mental object. This means that such patients cannot form symbols, cannot synthesize objects or combine words; they can only agglomerate or juxtapose them. The attack on language sometimes manifests itself as depriving words of their meaning. This is a real stripping. In synthesis, we are dealing with the destruction both of the language that is formed and of its matrix. These processes are the main factors in the differentiation of the psychotic and non-psychotic parts of the personality. The sadistic attacks on the matrix of thought and language together with the pathological projective identification of the fragments will cause increasing divergences between these two parts of the personality until eventually the separation will be felt as irreconcilable.

The patient dominated by the psychotic part of his personality feels he is a prisoner of his mental state. He is unable to liberate himself because he feels he lacks the apparatus of consciousness of reality that represents as much a key for escape as the liberty he is longing for. The fantasy of being incarcerated is intensified when he feels surrounded by the menacing presence of the evacuated fragments. Any attempt at synthesis will be very difficult; the patient can condense the objects but cannot correlate them (see chapter 6).

The predominance of the psychotic part of the personality is more obvious in the schizophrenic.

Language is used by the schizophrenic in different forms. He tends to resort to action on occasions when other people would use thoughts, and to use omnipotent thought when facing those problems that could be solved through action. In the first case he uses pathological projective identification to deal with words as concrete things or else tries to dissociate the mind of the analyst, by suggesting incompatible interpretative possibilities so as to obstruct understanding. The schizophrenic patient makes use of a "beta screen" (see chapter 3), to deposit in the analyst the "beta elements" that will elicit from him the specific answers the patient is looking for. These responses are not totally explained by the classical theory of countertransference.

As verbal thoughts depend on the elaboration of the depressive position, they involve greater knowledge of psychic reality and confront the patient with the pain of depression and loss of objects. If at some stage of analysis the patient recovers his symbolic capacity because of the appearance of alpha elements and becomes aware that communication is disturbed by his incapacity to link words appropriately, he is apt to feel imprisoned in the analysis, the analyst, or his own mental state of madness. He feels that any progress confronts him with the pain of getting to know his "madness." But he does not dare to regress to his previous state because he is afraid of feeling imprisoned and without any hope of recovery. This is why he tries to resort again to pathological projective identification to place the feared words, the feared language, and the feared consciousness he has acquired inside the therapist. This dilemma is repeated over and over again in the course of a treatment.

When analyzing the evolution of the schizophrenic patient we can see that when he reintrojects the capacity for verbal thought he becomes aware of his psychic state and his hallucinations. His reaction may be a deterioration that sometimes requires his admission to hospital. He now knows that he is insane and full of hatred, and accuses the analyst for having driven him to recognize his insanity.

Clinical Transference Manifestations of the Psychotic Personality

"Attack on linking," "arrogance," "hallucinations," "reversion of the perspective," "static splitting," and "forced splitting."

In the psychotic patient we find a permanent attack on all the links with the analyst that could lead to progress in any direction. The consequence of the "attack on linking" leaves the patient deprived of the mental state he needs to establish a mental relationship of growth. The origin of this aggression can be traced back to the fantasized and primitive attacks on the breast and the penis, as described by M. Klein, in the paranoid-schizoid position. But the psychotic tends to attack repeatedly links with the object and between different aspects of his self, the links between internal and external reality and the apparatus that perceives these realities. As a consequence of these "attacks on linking," the psychotic part is left preeminently with apparently logical, almost mathematical relationships that are never emotionally reasonable. These surviving links are of a perverse, cruel, and sterile character and are associated with arrogance, stupidity, and curiosity.

In the psychotic personality, where the death instinct predominates, pride can become a feeling Bion calls *arrogance,* whereas in the non-psychotic personality, where the life instinct predominates, pride will manifest itself as self-respect. The association of arrogance with obstinate curiosity and stupidity, which sometimes manifests itself through hints, references, or attitudes, forms a triad that is important to detect clinically. Bion refers these feelings to the influence of an internal object with characteristics of the primitive "Super" ego that denies and obstructs the normal use of projective identification—the mechanism that is the prototype of all links. The appearance of these feelings, which do not necessarily occur simultaneously in a session or in clinical material, is an important indicator of the existence of a psychic disaster that can result in overt psychosis.

The psychotic patient does not seem to be able to dream, or at least he does not bring dreams into his analysis until the treatment is well on its way. This does not mean that a patient who does not bring dreams to analysis has to be diagnosed as psychotic. It is important to differentiate the use of repression of oneiric phenomena in the cases of forgetfulness of dreams in neurotic patients from the incapacity to dream (because of the absence or deficit of alpha function) that can be observed in the psychotic patient. When a psychotic patient says he has had a dream he is more likely to be referring to an hallucination he had during the night than to oneiric phenomena.

In fact, *hallucination* is another of the clinical symptoms that characterize the psychotic personality. It is a typical phenomenon caused by the evacuation into the external world of split-off parts of the personality through the organs of sense. When the split-off parts of the personality have been violently fragmented into minute particles, their evacuation does not produce an hallucination (in the usual sense of the word), as these parts are deprived of any objective sensorial component. Bion calls these hallucinations *invisible hallucinations* and adds that they are very difficult to detect clinically and are only suggested by a gesture, attitude, or muscular jerk in the patient. The concepts formulated on hallucinations and other manifestations of the psychotic personality are included in the wider category *transformations in hallucinosis* which the reader will find discussed in chapter 5.

Another clinical configuration that can become manifest in the psychotic personality is the phenomenon Bion calls *reversal of perspective*. This denomination was taken from a well-known experiment of perceptual psychology that consists of the observation of a print that can represent either a vase or two profiles. Bion uses this experiment as a model of all situations of insight in which the personality is able to switch from one point of view to another in relation to something that is taking place. This provides "binocular vision" and gives the basis for the confrontation and correlation so necessary to mental development. But reversal of perspective in Bion's sense is a complex pathological phenomenon in which the patient tends to remain in one perspective only, from which he "sees" the interpretations and the whole of his analysis. This attitude is not manifest; on the contrary, it hides behind an apparent agreement and understanding of the perspective shown him by the analyst.

Reversal of perspective is an active and intentional phenomenon that can turn a dynamic situation into a static one *(static splitting)*. All evolution is stopped through this mechanism that is an indication of psychic pain. The pain from which the patient protects himself may be that of acknowledging his "madness." If he fails in his method of obstructing and immobilizing the analysis by a reversal of perspective, he resorts to *fleeting and evanescent hallucinations* that consist in actively "seeing wrongly," "hearing wrongly," and "understanding wrongly."

We would like to mention another clinical manifestation of the psychotic personality: that of *forced splitting*. It is based on a particular type of splitting described by Bion and refers to the behavior of the infant who feels very intense

envy toward the gratifying breast, to the extent that he stops
sucking. To avoid starvation he will start sucking again at
the breast on the basis of an enforced dissociation between
the material (milk and physical well-being) and psychic
gratification (love, understanding, etc.). Patients who use
this kind of splitting fear the consequences of hatred and
envy and therefore avoid all kinds of feelings. They greedily
try to acquire material comfort without being able to enjoy
it, and they cannot recognize the existence of the human
beings on whom they depend for such benefits. They cannot
experience gratitude for interest and treat others like
inanimate objects.

Catastrophic Change in the Psychotic Crisis

In the previous chapter we included the concept of
catastrophic change, characterized by violence, subversion
of order, and invariance.

Catastrophic change is an inevitable moment in all
processes of evolution and growth, as will be seen in
chapters 4 and 6; but we refer here to the particular type of
catastrophic change that appears in the analysis of certain
regressive *borderline* personalities with a predominantly
psychotic structure. In the analysis of a patient with these
characteristics, evolution is slow and difficult and may on
occasions undergo a psychotic crisis. This crisis, which in the
best of cases will be contained and controlled in the setting
of the analytic situation, can overflow this setting and erupt
noisily in the outside world. The crisis itself, whether
contained or not in the framework of the treatment, is
considered by Bion an example of catastrophic change.
Naturally, the analyst must pay special attention to the
emotional reactions that appear during the sessions, trying
to determine if his own pathology participates in a situation
that is dangerous and difficult for both.

The change that takes place is catastrophic in the restricted sense of an event that determines a subversion of order or system of things; it is catastrophic because it arouses feelings of disaster in the participants and because it appears abruptly and violently.

In the case of a controlled psychotic crisis, the elements that configurate catastrophic change are less evident and, unless one keeps them in mind, can even go unnoticed, in which case they may be detected in the transformation of the patient's attitude, in the context of the verbal and non-verbal material, and in the effect it has on the analyst (anxiety, preoccupation, dreams related to the transference problems, etc.). If the psychotic crisis is confined to the analytic treatment without repercussion or participation of external agents, and is gradually overcome, the catastrophic change will allow genuine progress in the integration of the personality. At other times the psychotic crisis can express itself with greater violence and can overflow the limits of the analytic task. Instead of its being restricted to the exclusive participation of the analytic couple, one may find the family intervening in the analysis of the patient by means of telephone calls, requests for admission into hospital, mobilization of psychiatrists, lawyers, etc. Bion points out the difficulty the analyst has in maintaining the psychoanalytic vertex in very disturbing circumstances that carry as much risk for the patient as they do for himself.

He points out the usefulness of distinguishing the invariants between the precatastrophic and the postcatastrophic stage. For example, in the case of a borderline patient with hypochondriacal symptoms, violence in the precatastrophic stage seems restricted to a theoretical level. In frank contrast to this, in the postcatastrophic stage violence becomes obvious in an explosive way and provokes reactions in the analyst and other people of his environment through "waves of expansion." The emotion is clearly externalized and the change takes place abruptly through an evident disturbance of the established order that neither patient nor analyst can avoid. Invariance can be detected, for example, in the fact that external factors in the form of anxious relatives, psychiatrists, and applications for admission and nurses correspond to the same internal factors (hypochondriacal pains and internal objects) that in the precatastrophic stage tried to protect the patient from the catastrophic change (psychotic crisis).

Notes

1. W. R. Bion, *Second Thoughts,* Heinemann, London, 1967.
2. S. Freud, The interpretation of dreams, S.E. 5.
3. These functions were described by Freud in his paper "Formulations on the two principles of mental functioning" (S.E. 12); they correspond to the functions of consciousness linked to the sense organs: notation, attention, judgment, thought, etc.
4. M. Klein, "Notes on some schizoid mechanisms," in *Developments in Psychoanalysis,* Hillary House, New York, 1952.
5. As L. Grinberg describes in his *Culpa y depresion* (Guilt and Depression) 2nd ed., Paidos, Buenos Aires, 1972.

Chapter 3

THOUGHT

Origin and Nature of Thinking: Theory of the Functions • Importance of Models in Psychoanalytic Theory and Technique: Their Application to the Theory of Thought • A Theory of Thought— "Apparatus to Think Thoughts": The Container-Contained Model and the Model of the Dynamic Interaction Between the Paranoid-Schizoid Position and the Depression Position • The Grid

The development, nature and contents of thoughts have from their primitive origins given place to a great number of studies carried out by psychologists, philosophers, linguists, and others.

Freud was the first to consider disturbances of thought from the psychoanalytic point of view. Throughout his work one can see the importance he attaches to unconscious fantasy and desire in the genesis, evolution, and content of thoughts. In *Formulations on the Two Principles of Mental Functioning*[1] he establishes the evacuative origin of thought, pointing out that it provides a means of restricting motor discharge and of relieving the increase of tension produced by delaying such discharge.

There are certain significant paragraphs which we feel would be useful to reproduce here: "The increased significance of external reality heightened the importance, too, of the sense organs that are directed towards the external world, and of the *consciousness* attached to them. Consciousness now learned to comprehend sensory quali-

ties in addition to the qualities of pleasure and displeasure.
. . . A special function was instituted which had periodically
to search the external world, in order that its data might be
familiar already if an urgent internal need should arise - the
function of *attention*."

"A new function was now allotted to motor discharge,
which, under the dominance of the pleasure principle, had
served as a means of unburdening the mental apparatus of
accretions of stimuli, and which had carried out this task by
sending innervations into the interior of the body (leading to
expressive movements and the play of features and to
manifestations of affect). Motor discharge was now
employed in the appropriate alteration of reality; it was
converted into action."

"Restraint upon motor discharge (upon action), which
then became necessary, was provided by means of the
process of thinking, which was developed from the
presentation of ideas. Thinking was endowed with characteristics which made it possible for the mental apparatus to
tolerate an increased tension of stimulus while the process of
discharge was postponed."

"For this purpose the conversion of freely displaceable
cathexes into *bound* cathexes was necessary, and this was
brought about by means of raising the level of the whole
cathectic process. *It is probable that thinking was originally
unconscious, in so far as it went beyond mere ideational
presentations and was directed to the relations between
impressions of objects, and that it did not acquire further
qualities perceptible to consciousness, until it became
connected with verbal residues*" (our italics).

It is significant to show that already at that time, in 1911,
Freud had pointed out that the beginning of dominance by
the reality principle is synchronous with the development of
an ability to think and thus bridge the frustrating gap
between the moment a need is felt and the point at which
appropriate action satisfies it.

Bion approached the study of the disturbances of thought through his experience of psychoanalytic practice. He looked at these disturbances as they appeared in the consulting room, in their multiple verbal and preverbal manifestations, in his communication with his patient. It is important not to lose sight of this fact, especially when at different times in the evolution of his ideas we find conceptualizations that are apparently detached from the psychoanalytic field and that seem more appropriate to epistemological or philosophical discussions. This happens, for example, when he postulates the existence of a "thought" is true as long as it is not formulated by a thinker. The intervention of the thinker automatically determines that the formulated thoughts becomes false expressions without necessarily being lies. We shall come back to these problems in chapter 6.

We shall now consider Bion's ideas about the process of thinking, about the evolution and transformation of thoughts and their uses at different levels in normal and seriously disturbed individuals.

Origin and Nature of Thinking:
Theory of Functions

Bion reformulated the existing theories about the process of thinking, postulating original concepts based on the consideration that "thinking" is a function of the personality which arises from the interaction of a variety of factors. In order to be able to develop his hypothesis he proposed a "theory of functions" which, articulated with the use of models, can be applied to analytic situations of different kinds, giving psychoanalytic theory and practice a greater flexibility. Bion uses the terms *function* and *factor* to define characteristics of the functions of the personality, without the stricter sense in which these terms are used in mathematics or symbolic logic (see chapter 1). In particular the "theory of functions" and the theory of "alpha-function" must be considered instruments in the psychoanalytic task which allow the analyst to work without having prematurely to propose new theories.

The area of investigation in which he applies the concept of "alpha-function" (intentionally devoid of meaning) includes thought processes as they manifest themselves in their end products, such as gestures, words, or more complex formulations. The theory of alpha-function includes the hypotheses (factors) that explain how these processes are produced and can be applied to the study and understanding of the capacity to think and of disturbances of thought. In his clinical practice the therapist can observe the different functions operating in the verbal and nonverbal behavior of his patient and can deduce the factors that play a part in each of them. Factors are elements of a function; the theories and hypotheses that appear as factors must be expressed and applied with rigorous precision.

Some functions can at the same time be factors of other functions which operate at more complex levels of the patient's reactions. As an example of a formulation we could say that certain characteristics observed in the behavior of a patient correspond to an "excess of projective identification" and "excess of bad objects" that are the fixed factors of the function of that patient's personality.

The theory of alpha-function postulates the existence of a function of the personality—*alpha-function*—which operates on sense impressions and on perceived emotional experiences, transforming them into alpha-elements. These, unlike the perceived impressions, can be used in new processes of transformation, for storing, for depression, etc. Alpha-elements are, then, those sense impressions and emotional experiences transformed into visual, auditory, olfactory, or other images in the mental domain. They are used in the formation of dream thoughts, unconscious thinking during wakefulness, dreams, and memories. Bion calls *beta-elements* those sense impressions and emotional experiences that are not transformed. These elements are not appropriate for thinking, dreaming, remembering, or exercising intellectual functions usually related to the psychic apparatus. These elements are experienced as things-in-themselves (viz. Kant) and are generally evacuated through projective identification.

Although it may seem obvious, we want to stress the fact that alpha- and beta-elements are theoretical terms which allow us to explain certain clinical facts and are not therefore elements that can be observed in analytic practice.

Bion also proposes the term *contact barrier* for the group formed by the proliferation of alpha elements that cohere and demarcate contact and separate between conscious and unconscious with a selective passage of elements from one to the other. This contact barrier, being in a constant process of formation, performs the function of a semipermeable membrane which separates mental phenomena into two groups. In this way, it provides the capacity to sleep or be awake, to be conscious or unconscious, and to have a notion of the past and future.

The *contact barrier* can be compared with the function of dreaming as protecting sleep; it prevents fantasies and endopsychic stimuli from interference by a realistic view. In turn it protects contact with reality, avoiding its distortion by emotions of internal origin.

Even though we are dealing with a field of abstractions, Bion proposes to consider the contact barrier as a structure in order to facilitate its understanding. It would thus be a part of the mental apparatus produced by alpha-function.

In the context of the same theory, Bion introduces another concept—*the beta-element screen*—which he uses to explain those mental states in which there is no differentiation between conscious and unconscious, sleep and wakefulness. Analogous to the contact barrier, the beta-screen is formed of beta-elements, and these beta-elements, considered things-in-themselves, do not have the capacity to relate to each other. Therefore, the beta-screen is a product of the agglomeration of beta-elements, more like an agglutination than an integration. Nevertheless, these can achieve a certain coherence that manifests itself by provoking certain emotional responses in the object, which can be clinically observed.[2] The contact barrier is the basis for the normal relation to reality, and to the internal and external world, while the beta-screen is a characteristic of the psychotic part of the personality.

The contact barrier can be destroyed, in which case alpha-elements are divested of all their characteristics and become beta-elements that are joined by residues of the ego and the superego, which then form bizarre objects (see chapter 2).

Let us stop for a moment to think about the fascinating model Bion proposes for the understanding of the normal and pathological functioning of the human mind. Alpha-elements, contact barrier, beta-elements, and beta-screen will be the result of the vicissitudes of sensations and emotions arising from immediate experience, and will depend on the degree and mode of operation of the alpha-function. Patients who have a serious disturbance in their capacity to think are considered, according to this model, as having a deteriorated or underdeveloped alpha-function that fails to produce alpha-elements. Instead there will be a predominance of beta-elements that underlies a tendency to act and to use concrete thought owing to an incapacity for symbolization and abstraction. The deficit of alpha-function determines the state of certain psychotic patients who "cannot go to sleep and cannot wake up." Undoubtedly this deficit is responsible for the inability to dream or to remember dreams that we so often observe in our clinical experience with psychotic patients. It is an undeniable fact that psychotic patients have an enormous difficulty in dreaming, which coincides with their disturbance of thought. When these patients report "dreams," we can assume they are not dreams composed of dream thoughts formed of alpha-elements, but rather are hallucinatory phenomena or what Bion more precisely calls "a transformation hallucinosis" (see chapter 5), characterized by an overwhelming presence of beta-elements. The psychotic patient in analysis may acquire alpha-elements and therefore a capacity to dream, but he may not have fully recovered this alpha-function and is therefore still unable to think. In this case he uses projective identification to "treat" his thoughts and dreams. Finally, when he has improved considerably, he will not only be able to dream but also to think, thanks to the development and consolidation of the apparatus for thinking his thoughts, as we shall see later on.

Importance of Models in Psychoanalytic Theory and Technique: Their Application to the Theory of Thought

The inclusion of models in the psychoanalytic field can very often be advantageous from the point of view of their operativity. Bion gives the basis and explains the reasons he thinks their use convenient, pointing out their flexibility in contrast to the rigidity of theories. On the other hand, if the analyst can build appropriate models he will avoid falling into the tendency to create new ad hoc theories every time he confronts serious difficulties in his work. The model makes it possible to find a correspondence between the specific problems the patients present and the main body of psychoanalytic theory. The models may be suggested by clinical material, and they perform a very valuable function so long as they are not mistaken for theories. The use of models is ephemeral, as they can be discarded as soon as they have fulfilled their purpose or failed to do so. Should they prove useful on different occasions, one could then consider the possibility of transforming them into theories.

The use of models is also helpful in restoring a sense of the concrete to an investigation that may have lost touch with its origins due to the abstraction used throughout it.

The model is built with elements related to sense experience and allows the establishment of a bridge between the clinically observed facts and the abstract theory or theories with which the analyst approaches these facts. The quality of concreteness, which is derived from the senses, has the virtue of limiting excessive abstraction during an investigation; but it involves the risk of excessive concretization associated to the causal and narrative quality inherent in the model which provides the conviction of a "concrete reality."

When the analyst builds his model in clinical practice, he must also be aware of the model used by the patient and must bring it out into the open. The model used by the analyst must allow him to arrive at an interpretation of the facts that are presented for his scrutiny. The analyst creates the model as a step in the elaboration of the interpretation, and it is not in itself an interpretation. From the point of reference of the patient's material, the analyst must determine why it is being produced and what the correct interpretation would be. For example, he compares what the patient tells him with the theory of the Oedipus complex. The model brings about two groups of ideas: those related to the patient's material and those related to the body of psychoanalytic theory. Bion also points out the analogy between the role played by the myth in the group context of society and that of the model in the scientific theory of the individual.

The more complex the problem the greater the need to use appropriate models, as happens in studying the characteristics of mental growth. Let us assume that the analyst is treating a patient with serious thought disturbances. He will then need a model that corresponds to the way of thinking of the particular patient, and it would be useful for him to have his own model and theory about the process of thinking, which he can then compare with the models built by the patient. The theory of thought that Bion proposes, together with the use of certain models, tries to clarify some of these problems. (See Appendix § 3.)

A Theory of Thought—"Apparatus to Think Thoughts": The Container-Contained Model and the Model of the Dynamic Interaction Between the Paranoid Schizoid Position and the Depressive Position

The theory of thought formulated by Bion starts by proposing that thoughts exist and give rise to an apparatus for manipulating them called thinking. The activity we know as thinking was in its origin a procedure for unburdening the psyche of an excessive and overwhelming amount of stimuli. According to Bion, thoughts are considered genetically and epistemologically prior to the capacity to think. In the earlier stages of development thoughts are nor more than sense impressions and very primitive emotional experiences ("proto-thoughts") related to the concrete experience of a thing-in-itself (as Kant defines what is unknowable in the object).

When using the term *thought,* Bion refers to thoughts, preconceptions, conceptions, thoughts proper, and concepts.

In order to understand the implications of each of these categories, we shall use as a model the relationship between the mother and her baby. For the baby, the taking in of milk, warmth, and love is equated with incorporating a good breast. The baby, which Bion assumes has an innate preconception of the breast, is not, however, aware of its need for the good breast. Driven by hunger, it experiences an unsatisfied need (the bad breast) which it tries to get rid of.

For Bion, all needed objects are bad objects; they are needed because they are not possessed. Otherwise there would be no deprivation. Therefore the primitive thoughts or proto-thoughts are bad objects the baby needs to get rid of.

The real experience with the actual breast provides the baby an opportunity to get rid of this bad breast. The mother provides not only food but is a container for all the unpleasant feelings (bad breast) of the baby. The elimination of the bad breast into the mother constitutes the evacuation of a beta-element through the mechanism of projective identification. In terms of the theory of thought, Bion suggests that in this case we have a complex situation. On the one hand we can say that a *preconception* (innate expectation of the breast analagous to Kant's concept of "empty thought") has mated with a *realization* (real experience with the breast) giving birth to a *conception.* When the perconception is not found in the real breast there is a combination of a preconception and a frustration (a situation which Bion calls negative realization, or, in other terms, is equivalent to a combination between a preconception which can give place to the appearance of "thought").

It is important to point out, in relation to this last point, that Bion considers *tolerance of frustration* an innate factor in the baby's personality, which is therefore of great importance for the process of thought formation and the capacity to think.

When faced with frustration, the personality has several options. If intolerance of frustration is great, the personality tries to *avoid it* by evacuating beta-elements (things in themselves), while an adequate tolerance of frustration sets in motion the mechanisms which will tend to *modify it,* which, in the case of the baby, results in the production of alpha-elements and thoughts that represent the thing-in-itself.

The capacity to form thoughts will then depend on the child's capacity to tolerate frustration. If this capacity is sufficient, the "no-breast" becomes a thought and the "apparatus for thinking thoughts" develops.

Intolerance of frustration makes him avoid frustration instead of modifying it, and what should be a thought becomes a bad object indistinguishable from a thing-in-itself and fit only for evacuation.

Thinking for Bion designates two processes that are actually different: there is a thinking that gives place to thoughts, and a thinking that consists of using epistemologically preexisting thoughts. For the latter form of thinking it is necessary for one to differentiate within the psyche an apparatus for thinking thoughts.

Two main mechanisms take part in the formation of this apparatus: the first is represented by the dynamic relation between something which is projected, the *contained* ($\male$) and an object which contains it, container ($\female$). The second is represented by the dynamic relation between the paranoid-schizoid position and the depressive position (Ps $\leftrightarrow$ D).

An apparatus for thinking thoughts is formed in the infant's mind with the intervention of these mechanisms. At first, the baby repeatedly internalizes good experiences of its relation with the mother. This means that the baby has internalized a "happy couple" formed by a receptive and metabolizing mother (container), through the alpha-function of the feelings projected by the baby, and by the baby who, through projective identification, has placed his various emotions (contained) in her.

What is the possible fate of these evacuated contents? In favorable circumstances these contents are evacuated into an external breast which is real at that moment (the mother who is preparing to feed the infant and perceives the baby's need within herself). The mother who functions as an effective container of the infant's sensations can successfully transform hunger into satisfaction, pain into pleasure, loneliness into company, fear of dying into peacefulness. This capacity of the mother to be open to the baby's projected need Bion calls the capacity for *reverie*.

We will now deal with the second mechanism: that of the dynamic interaction between the paranoid-schizoid position and the depressive position (Ps ↔ D). M. Klein described the paranoid-schizoid position as the situation of the baby who, exposed to the impact of external reality and to the anxiety provoked by his death instinct, uses the mechanisms of dissociation, denial, omnipotence, idealization and projective identification to defend himself. The result is a dissociation of the objects into idealized and persecutory objects. The extreme operation of these mechanisms can lead to situations of dispersal and fragmentation of the ego and the objects (splitting).

In the depressive position there is a process of integration of the dissociation we have just described, with the appearance of feelings of ambivalence. There are also moments of depressive integration in the paranoid-schizoid position.

Bion conceptualizes the moments of disintegration and integration as a constant oscillation between both situations and symbolizes this relation with the sign Ps ↔ D, which notes what Poincaré described as the discovery of the *selected fact*.

A selected fact is an emotion or an idea which gives coherence to what is dispersed and introduces order into disorder. The selected fact is the name of an emotional experience, of a feeling of discovery of coherence, and can be expressed by the name of an element which is used to particularize it.

In the formation and use of thoughts, as in the integration of the object, both processes— ♀ , ♂ and Ps ↔ D—operate together and one cannot ascribe more importance to one than to the other.

Schematically, and at the risk of being repetitive, we shall summarize the experiences that lead to the formation of the capacity to think thoughts as follows:

1. The baby cries because he is hungry but his mother is not present to satisfy his need. In this case we have the union of a preconception with a negative realization (absence of the breast). The infant experiences it as the presence of the bad breast or no-breast, indistinguishable from a thing-in-itself or beta-element, and tends to evacuate it.

2. The baby cries because he is hungry and is satisfied by the gratifying contact with the mother's breast. We can represent this situation as the union of a preconception (innate expectation of the breast) with a realization (presence of the gratifying good breast) which gives place to a conception, characterized by its sense perceptual quality.

3. An evacuation of the bad breast into the real external breast takes place through a realistic projective identification. The mother, with her capacity for reverie, transforms the unpleasant sensations linked to the "bad breast" and provides relief for the infant who then reintrojects the mitigated and modified emotional experience, i.e. reintrojects an alpha-function, a non-sensual aspect of the mother's love.

4. If an infant has an innate tolerance of frustration and his envy is not too intense when confronting a new experience of negative realization, he will become aware of the first notion of the absence of the object and frustration (equivalent to a "problem to be solved"); that is what Bion calls "thought." This thought will mate with a new realization and give place to the matrix of a new thought, and so on.

5. If an infant has an innate intolerance to frustration which stems from very intense envy (in the sense M. Klein[3] gives this term), he will tend to avoid frustration through a hypertrophic development of the apparatus for projective identification, making the latter more omnipotent and less realistic (without taking into account the presence of the real object-container). The infant will then develop a type of personality that will not form the apparatus for thinking thoughts. Instead he will use continual evacuative discharge by projective identification with the characteristics described earlier on. His mind will function like a muscle which continuously discharges beta-elements.

It would be helpful to mention that the container-contained (♀ ♂) model can be used to represent successful or unsuccessful projective identification. An infant who cries because he is afraid of dying will find a loving and understanding mother who picks him up, smiles at him, and says, "Well, well it's not all that bad." He calms down because he could, according to the model, put his fear of dying into the mother through projective identification, and this fear is now returned to him in a milder, more tolerable fear. A second example would be that of a mother who reacts with anxiety and lack of understanding and says: "I don't know what is wrong with this child," putting an emotional distance between herself and the crying baby. The mother has rejected the infant's projection and returns to him the unmodified fear of dying. A third example would be that of a very disturbed, maybe psychotic baby, or of a very disturbed mother. In this case the fantasy underlying the projective identification is that the mother, instead of detoxifying the fear of dying which is projected by the child, acts as a bad object that strips the baby's projection of its meaning in a greedy, envious, and hostile way, and returns to him a *nameless dread* through the introjection of an object with these characteristics. This last example would correspond to the model "minus container-contained" (− ♀♂); see chapter 6.

From the beginning of life, the individual's psyche has to choose between two possible alternatives. These alternatives will depend on the quality or nature of the experience of primitive thoughts and the degree of evolution reached by the apparatus for thinking. If proto-thoughts are considered "undesirable excrescences" and the "apparatus for thinking" is not sufficiently developed, the primitive thoughts will be evacuated as beta-elements through a hypertrophic projective identification. If these proto-thoughts can be accepted as "problems for solving," there will be an awareness of the state of deprivation they imply (as these are unsolved problems).

This tolerance of the pain of frustration and the convenient reinforcement of the "apparatus for thinking" by the successful functioning of ♀ ♂ and Ps ↔ D mechanisms allow an action to be triggered off in the internal and external world that will tend to modify the state of deprivation. According to Bion this transformation into action involves a number of steps called, respectively, *publication, communication* and *commonsense.*

As we have just seen, the development of thought and thinking depends on the interplay of two fundamental groups of factors. There are innate factors (tolerance or intolerance of frustration) and environmental factors (the mother's capacity for *reverie),* which together determine the development and further evolution of the capacity to think, which, in the case of a positive evolution, will increase with the formation of concepts, abstractions, hypotheses, systems, etc. The capacity to combine thoughts to create symbols and language involves processes in which *correlation, publication,* and *communication* will have a predominant role. This development corresponds to the nonpsychotic part of the personality. At the opposite pole is the psychotic personality, unable to represent or to use symbols and revealed to the observer through hallucinations, acting out, lack of coherence, etc.

Publication corresponds in its origin to a specific function of thought which allows sense data to become conscious, but Bion prefers to use this word for the operations which convey the data of the internal world to the external world. *Communication,* on the other hand, originally takes place by realistic projective identification and develops as a part of the social capacity of the individual; the fact that certain phenomena are in a constant conjunction is transmitted by communication. If this conjunction of data is harmonious, it will lend a sense of truth.

The Grid

We shall now refer to the use of an instrument proposed by Bion to help the analyst think about problems arising in psychoanalytic practice. It is a method of recording, comparable to that used by the mathematician for notation, communication, and further elaboration of the different discoveries and observations which have taken place, even in the case where the object is absent.

This instrument, the "grid," is not only useful to add to the methods of observation but is in itself a product of the observation. It comprises a series of categories Bion called *elements* of psychoanalysis.

These elements are functions of the personality formed by factors (with the specific meanings already determined for these terms). Bion proposes to consider the elements as phenomena observable through their primary and secondary qualities and conceived as having dimensions in the domain of sense, myth, and passion.

The first dimension refers to a sense experience which

follows "common sense" criteria. Bion uses *common sense* to denote the non-sensory impression, which can be compared with that obtained in the sensory area when an object or a characteristic of the object can be confirmed by two or more senses of one person or by only one sense of many persons. The extension in the domain of myth is related to an elaboration of certain aspects included in the personal equipment available to each analyst and has been compared by Bion to the use of models in psychoanalytic practice. Finally, the term *passion* applies to the evidence that at least two minds are present and that an emotion arises between these two minds which is experienced with intensity and warmth, but without violence.

The elements of psychoanalysis constitute ideas or feelings represented by one category of the grid. The formation of these categories has been achieved by means of two coordinates: a vertical one, with the letters A, B, . . . H, represents the increasing degree of complexity acquired by thought and corresponds to the genetic axis; a horizontal axis represents the *use* given the different categories formulated by the vertical axis and is numbered 1, 2, 3, . . . n. This horizontal axis is incomplete in order to show that the series may be extended indefinitely beyond what is indicated, according to eventual uses still to be discovered. It is divided into columns according to criteria created by Bion, to indicate the domain of learning through experience. The relation between the two axes delineates a category which implies a comprehensive area of information about what is formulated.

The purpose of the table is to categorize formulations. By formulations we understand both the most simple elements and the most elaborate constructions. A word, a gesture, a movement can be formulated, as well as any event taking place within or outside the analytic session. Everything that is part of the communication between the analyst and the analysand—a certain personality, an article, a book—may be included in any one of the forty-eight categories of the grid.

The *psychoanalytic objects,* which have the dimensions of sense, mythology, and psychoanalytic theory must show the characteristic features of rows B, C, and G, unlike those elements which can be included only in a single category of the grid. An analytic object relates to the elements as a molecule to atoms.

We can consider the first two rows of the vertical axis together; the beta-elements and the alpha-elements are destined to show different levels of thought. They are not clinically observable but are theoretical terms useful for thinking and talking about the different phenomena. The beta-elements are primitive and represent not thoughts but things-in-themselves (Kant). In them, there is no differentiation between what is animate and inanimate, subject and object, internal world and external world, symbol and that which is symbolized. Also, as they are saturated, they cannot be used as preconceptions. They can be evacuated only through projective identification. The alpha-elements, which are a result of the operation of alpha-function on sense-impressions and emotional experiences, can be stored as incipient thoughts. They allow the individual to have dreams on the basis of what Freud called "dream thoughts." Row C represents the phenomena formed by dream thoughts, visual images, dreams, hallucinations, and all the ideas combined in a narrative form as, for example, private and public myths. Row D corresponds to the *preconception*; it is a mental state of expectation which is adapted to receive a restricted range of phenomena of which one example could be the infant's expectation of the breast. If this state is integrated with a realization that has a sense and perceptual predominance, there arises a *conception* which occupies Row E. The *concept* defines and characterizes row F and derives from a conception by a process of abstraction which has freed it from the sensory-perceptual elements. It represents a category for already existing enunciations as, for example, psychoanalytic theories, general scientific theories, laws of nature, etc. Row G represents the *scientific deductive systems.* These are combinations of concepts and hypotheses or systems of hypotheses logically related to each other. Finally in row H is found the *algebraic calculus,* in which different signs can be brought together according to certain rules of combination, as in mathematics. All the rows, with the exception of the first one, represent categories of formulations which are not saturated; i.e. they are able to accumulate meaning. The last rows (G and H) do not have much clinical application.

The horizontal axis refers to the possible uses of the different categories we have just mentioned. First is presented a column called *definitory hypothesis.* It brings together the facts that have been previously discovered and are in constant conjunction. At first these formulations have no meaning; they are merely significatory and can be used simply to avoid the loss of emotional experience through dispersion. The definitory hypothesis has two negative qualities: first is the fact that in designating something with a certain name all that is not included in the designation is excluded; second is that the name is a representation and not a thing-in-itself. The ability to tolerate the negative qualities of the definitory hypothesis implies the ability to tolerate frustration. Column 2 corresponds to false formulations that are known to be false with the intention of counteracting the formulations which can generate anxiety or the developments which imply catastrophic change. Column 3 comprises the categories used to record an event and has the functions of *notation* and *memory.* Column 4 represents what Freud described as *attention* and free-floating attention; it is used to probe the environment and is important for discrimination. Column 5 is used for those formulations that allow the exploration to be directed to a particular object. It has also been called the column of *inquiry* or of Oedipus, because of the insistence with which he carried out his investigation. Finally, column 6 represents the use of thoughts related to *action* or to transformations into action. Columns 3 to 5 define a spectrum of attention that goes from memory and desire through free-floating attention to a greater degree of specificity. Columns 2 and 6 and row C will need further extensions to encompass the wide range of complex phenomena presenting themselves for observation.

To place any formulation on this grid, it is necessary to take into account genetic level and the use given to it. The same formulation, word, phrase, etc. can be placed in any category of the grid, provided the observer has discriminated its level of complexity and use. We shall take as an example the formulation of a patient who tries to attack his relationship with the analyst; this would be an acting out through evacuation of beta-elements and corresponds therefore to A6. On the other hand, acting may be a means of communication that tends to provoke greater understanding in the analyst and therefore it would correspond to the category D6 or E6. The interpretations formulated in the analytic session, insofar as they are comparable to actions in other forms of human behavior, can also be placed in this column, for example in F6.

The grid must not be considered a rigid instrument. On the contrary, it should be used before or after the session but never during the session. The forty-eight categories are not exhaustive or exclusive. They can be replaced by better categories more appropriate to the phenomena one wants to note. It can be very useful for the analyst who works on his own and is not exposed to critical comments on his work to test either the analytic theories he uses or those he has to supervise himself. Bion also suggests that each analyst could construct his own grid.

The function of the grid is also to facilitate communication between analysts; in applying the model proposed by Bion, it is possible to refer to the patient's material or to a myth by indicating its category on the grid, avoiding in this way having to explain the origin and uses of the material, myth, or dream under discussion. This resource is used by Bion in many of his books and it is therefore necessary for the reader to familiarize himself with the terminology created by the use of the grid.

Notes

1. S. Freud, Formulations on the two principles of mental functioning, S.E. 12.
2. This hypothesis has many points in common with the concept developed by one of us under the rubric *projective counteridentification*. See L. Grinberg, "On some problems of psychoanalytic technique determined by projective identification and projective counter-identification." *Revista de Psicoanalisis* 13, 1956; "Psychopathology or projective identification, projective counteridentification and counter-transference," *Revista de Psicoanalisis* 20, 1963.
3. M. Klein, "Envy and Gratitude," in *Envy and Gratitude*, Tavistock, London, 1957.

TRANSFORMATIONS

In this chapter a new perspective is introduced for the understanding of problems in the area of thought, psychosis, and groups through the term *transformations.* Terms like *invariance, transformations,* and others that already have a meaning in philosophy, mathematics, and other disciplines will now be used to talk specifically about problems in psychoanalysis. This approach may at times seem strange. Bion himself says in the first chapter of his book *Transformations*: "any apparent strangeness lies in the method of approach and not in the experience described."[1] In the present chapter the reader will find a simplified explanation of the approach, together with some examples of its application to psychoanalytic problems.

Transformations and Invariance—
Groups of Transformations

Transformation means a change of form. The concept is often used in very different contexts and is applicable to many situations. For instance, we say that under certain circumstances water is transformed into steam; we consider a map as a transformed version of a geographical area and a painting representing a landscape as being a product of a series of transformations. In some branches of science the concept of transformation is used more systematically, as in projective geometry, in the theory of groups, and in transformational grammar. Psychoanalytic theory also makes use of the concept of transformation. It considers the manifest content of a dream as a result of a process (dream work) which has transformed latent ideas into visual images; psychical conflict after transformation expresses itself as symptoms, and the transference is a transformed version of repressed infantile situations which are repeated in the relationship with the therapist.

Bion proposes a theory of transformations that refers not so much to the main body of psychoanalytic theory but to the practice of psychoanalysis and to *psychoanalytic observation* in particular. He draws our attention to the fact that we are *permanently observing and performing transformations*. The patient's associations formulated into words are a product of a transformation of thoughts and emotions; these thoughts and emotions refer to events (external and internal, past and present) of which they are in turn transformations. In the same way the psychoanalytic interpretation is a verbal transformation of the analyst's thoughts and these are part of a process of transformation of the emotional experience during contact with the patient.

In all the examples presented so far, and whenever one speaks of transformation, it is possible to distinguish or assume an *initial fact or state, a process of transformation* carried out by a certain technique and under certain conditions, and an *end product* which is the result of the process.

Bion proposes the *"O" sign for the original fact, "T" for* the transformation, "T-alpha (T α)" for the process, and

"T-beta (T β)" for the end product. Each of these signs and their application will be discussed in greater detail later on. It is also important to determine the *context* in which the transformation takes place: for example, if it is in the domain of physical objects, of language, or of art. Water, as an initial state of fact of a process of transformation, will give different end products according to the context in which the transformation takes place; in a physical medium it will be transformed into ice or steam; if the context is verbal it could be transformed into a symbol or a word; if it is art, into a painting, a musical piece, etc. In psychoanalysis it is important to determine the context in which transformations take place, be they the mind, the body, or the external world.

The concept of *invariance* is closely related to that of transformation and refers to that which remains unaltered by the process. Invariance allows recognition of the original thing in the end product of the transformation. In our previous example, invariance would reside in the molecular structure of the water; in the case of the word *water,* it would reside in the meaning. Thus invariance is closely bound to the particular context in which the transformation takes place and to the point of view from which the observer approaches the phenomenon.

Using the signs proposed by Bion, we may say that invariance refers to the unaltered aspects of 0 after the process of transformation (T α) is completed. The invariants allow the recognition in the end product (T β) of the original thing that has been transformed (0). The invariants will greatly depend on the technique employed to carry out the process of transformation (T α) and the degree of deformation which this implies.

An analogy taken from another field will illustrate these concepts. Let us assume a painter sees a landscape and paints it. The landscape, according to our terminology, will be 0; the painting, the end result of a series of transformations, T β . If, when we look at the painting we can recognize the landscape it represents, in spite of the big difference between a landscape and the pigments spread out on the canvas, it is because something has remained unaltered. That "something" is what we call *invariant*. The T α of the painter is the process that starts with his visual impression of the landscape and lasts until the painting is produced. It may be of importance to know the artist's technique is to correctly interpret the painting. Two painters belonging to different schools (for example, realism and impressionism) will represent the same landscape differently, and the detectable invariants will therefore also be different. In the theory of transformations, the methods and techniques employed to carry out the transformations are called *groups of transformations*.

In the field of psychoanalytic practice we can consider the patient's behavior in the session, his associations, gestures, etc., as being equivalent to the artist's painting—that is, T β or, to be more specific, T (patient) β of the facts (0) that he has transformed in a certain way. In this case also, we can assume that we can recognize in his report or behavior something of the original. In general, we agree that there are invariants in his thoughts and words which allow us to know what he is telling us; we try to discover and clarify the meanings of his behavior through the invariants detected by our observation. We may also be interested in knowing the techniques of transformation used by the patient—T (patient) α ; the context in which it takes place; and especially the emotional factors which take part in the process.

Bion distinguishes different groups of transformations in the mental area: *rigid motion transformations, projective transformations* and *transformations in hallucinosis*.

The events of the session are the O of the analyst's transformations. The patient's associations, his behavior, gestures, all that happens in the session is O for the analyst.

His mental processes correspond to T (analyst) α and his interpretation to T (analyst) β . The publication of clinical material will imply a new process of transformation, this time in a different context, with a different T β .

Psychoanalytic theories can be conceptualized as groups of transformations. The patient's material is interpreted in a certain way according to these theories. A Freudian and a Kleinian, given the same material, will give different interpretations, as each will detect and point to different invariants according to his theories. The clinical material presented in a scientific meeting will elicit T (Freudian analyst) β and T (Kleinian analyst) β , which are different but undoubtedly less different than the hypothetical interpretation of the same material made by a relative of the patient in question: T (lay relative) β .

We have already said that the processes of transformation are carried out in a person's mind, with different techniques. The same event can be transformed in different ways at different times or by different parts of the personality. It is important for the analyst to take into account that an end product (Tp β), for example a word, can be an adequate representation of a thought, a misrepresentation, or perhaps not a representation at all (in the common sense of the word), as may sometimes happen in the psychotic patient. In this case, words are used for evacuation and not as vehicles for meanings.

The grid designed by Bion (see chapter 3) allows us to categorize the ideas and expressions according to their levels of evolution and according to the ways they are used. The classification of different groups of transformations enriches the use of the grid and may lead to an improved version of it.

Transformations

Rigid Motion Transformations
and Projective Transformations

The terms *rigid motion transformation* and *projective transformation* are taken from projective geometry. We will briefly explain these terms as they are used in that field and try to transfer these concepts for use as models in the psychoanalytic field. Projective geometry studies the properties of the figures which remain invariant under different groups of transformations. These transformations may be variously projective, rigid motion, continuous motion, etc., and for each type of transformation there are different invariants. Projective transformations in a plane or in space are those which take place by projection and section. A projective transformation, then, transforms points into points and lines into lines and preserves their properties of incidence. It does not preserve the distance or the angles; these properties are not invariant in the group of projective transformations. Rigid transformations, such as transportation and rotation, leave the size and angles of the figures invariant; elemental Euclidean geometry studies the properties which remain invariant in this group of transformations.

Rigid motion transformations in the mind imply by analogy little deformation. They leave invariant more or less permanently certain meanings and other characteristics. The transformations of thoughts into words that represent them, according to codes that are common to most of the people who use the same language, are also rigid motion transformations. Their use, and the fact that the invariants are easily observed, allows the speaker to understand (transform) the meaning that is implied.

A clinical example taken from Bion's *Transformations*[2] illustrates the application of the rigid motion transformations (pp. 15–16). "The patient, a man of 40, married with one son, whose childhood was spent in a well-to-do professional family of father and mother with three older brothers, had complained of insomnia. The occasion was the last session before a weekend, and he commenced it by saying he had dreamt that a tiger and a bear were fighting. He felt dreadfully frightened less the animals in their ferocious maulings would stumble across him and kill him. He woke in dread, with a shout ringing in his ears. It was his own shout. The dream reminded him of a story by a famous big game shot; he could not remember the name of the man. The tiger who was well known to be the fiercest of animals was driven off its kill by a bear. But the bear had its nose bitten off. It made him shudder to think of it. (Here he screwed up his face and shuddered.) He could not think of any more. He went on after a pause: The girl he was once engaged to for a year had broken off the engagement because she wanted to be free to flirt with other men. It still made his blood boil. Pepper was the man she married. He was very fond of pepper himself. Pepper was hot stuff with the girls. So unlike himself who was always afraid of them. With his wife it was different, but she was dull. At this point he became confused and I omit the rest of the session."

The transcribed material lends itself easily to interpretation. The psychoanalytically trained reader can see that the weekend break could have been a stimulus for the dream and associations. The interpretation would depend on various factors, among them the data the analyst already has of the patient's analysis, the emotional climate of the session, etc.

To reformulate these situations in terms of the theory of transformations, the following question comes to the fore: what is O (patient)? In other terms, what is he talking about? A possible answer is that he is talking about the weekend break. If this assumption is adopted O (patient) will be the weekend break. In this particular case it can be reformulated on the basis of psychoanalytic theories about the primal scene, and one could then say that O (patient) is the primal scene, with associations that add shades of meaning to the understanding of what is taking place.

It might also be valuable to know what in the patient's state of mind might induce him to experience the weekend in a particular way, his Tp (α), i.e., as a frightening situation. If we assume that the transference plays a predominant role, T (patient) β is what the analyst would call the transference neurosis.

An aspect of transference phenomena important in the transformation is the tendency, described by Freud, to repeat some repressed event as current experience in action, rather than to remember it as a fragment of the past.[3] This transformation implies little deformation; the term *transference* as used by Freud is a model of the movement of feelings and ideas from one sphere of applicability to another.

When the analyst assumes that certain ideas and feelings which belong to infantile sexuality and the Oedipus complex are transported or transferred to the relationship with the therapist while preserving their coherence and structure, he is applying a model of rigid motion transformation to his understanding of the phenomena.

In summary, rigid motion transformations are considered to be a group of transformations or a technique of transformation in the area of emotions, thoughts, and words.

Insofar as the transformations carried out with this technique give a less distorted Tp than do other transformation techniques (projective transformations or transformations in hallucinosis), the analyst who listens to the patient will be able to reconstruct with less difficulty the process which goes from O to Tp and to interpret the material. Furthermore, in the case of rigid motion transformations, the analyst can, from his O analyst (Oa), discern the O patient (Op) (the weekend break in the previous example), as both O's when intersecting form an O common to both patient and analyst.

Another group of transformations in the mental area is called *projective transformations*. The model used here is that of a transformation which preserves the invariance of characteristics which differ from those of rigid motion transformations. In addition, it uses different methods of transformation.

Another fragment of clinical material, also taken from *Transformations,* can be used as an example of this type of transformation (pp. 19–20).

"The patient came in, but, though he had been attending for years, seemed uncertain what to do. 'Good morning, good morning, good morning. It must mean afternoon really. I don't expect anything can be expected today: this morning, I mean. This afternoon. It must be a joke of some kind. This girl left about her knickers. Well, what do you say to that? It's probably quite wrong, of course, but, well, I mean, what do *you* think?' He walked to the couch and lay down, bumping his shoulders down hard on the couch. 'I'm slightly anxious . . . I think. The pain has come back in my knee. You'll probably say it was the girl. After all, this picture is probably not very good as I told him but I should not have said anything about it. Mrs. X . . . thought I ought to go to Durham to see about, but then' and so on."

This material differs in many ways from the previous example. It is more complex and cannot be easily interpreted; it requires a reformulation that will contain a high degree of speculation. It is hard to tell what the patient is talking about or what O (patient) is. The Kleinian theories of splitting and projective identification can be applied in an attempt to clarify the mental state of the patient and his apparent difficulty in distinguishing between himself and the analyst. The difficulty in interpreting is mainly caused by the emotional climate of the session itself.

If one tries to understand this material on the assumption that the language used by the patient retains the habitual meanings, it will hardly be understood. Some progress can be made in understanding the material if it is assumed that the words are the product of non-habitual transformations and tend to transmit a meaning (TP β) that is the result of an emotional experience in which concepts, space, and time are used in a way different from the customary one.

The Kleinian theory of projective identification together with the theory of splitting can explain the patient's confusion and his apparent difficulty in distinguishing adequately between himself and the analyst. In our attempt to understand we assume that the transformations in the patient's mind have taken place through projection, dissociation, and projective identification, and that these processes continue during verbalization. It is clear that the end products of transformations of this type, since they result from processes that do not respect the time-space limits habitual to the non-psychotic personality, will have to be understood in a different way by the observer.

In projective transformations, events far removed from the session in time and space are considered either part of the session or aspects of the analyst's personality. "Distances and ages" are not respected but are intensely exaggerated and deformed in these transformations (what Bion calls "hyperbole").

While in rigid motion transformations the relation with O is relatively easy to establish because the invariants can be clearly detected, things are different in projective transformations. The invariants which correspond to Op and Oa differ widely.

When the non-psychotic part of the personality predominates, the theories commonly used by the analyst (his groups of transformations) will correspond to the rigid motion model. However, to understand the way in which the most primitive part of the mind functions, it is necessary for the analyst to use theories in which this other mode of transformation—more archaic and less logical—acquires meaning and thus facilitates clarification. Kleinian theories about primitive defense mechanisms allow an approach to this type of transformation.

Transformations in Hallucinosis

Bion describes a third type of transformation: *transformations in hallucinosis*. The end product of this process can be, among other things, an hallucination, and this may or may not manifest itself clinically in the patient. Behavior, language, and actions that characterize the way the psychotic part of the personality functions (see chapter 2) are expressions (in the context of the theory of transformations) of transformations in hallucinosis. For the observer, the difficulty in detecting and understanding this type of transformation is even greater than the one found in the example of projective transformations, as the analyst frequently has no access to the end product ($T \beta$). In chapter 5 the reader will find a more detailed discussion of the problems inherent in this type of transformation, as well as the specific method proposed by Bion to come in contact with them.

Transformations from "O" and in "O"

In the three groups of transformations described so far we have referred to processes of transformation that have a starting point in an initial experience or situation, categorized as O of the transformation.

The sign O now requires further classification. We have referred O to particular situations which are always related to some aspect of physical or psychic reality. We want to point out its unknowable character, as this is the sense Bion attributes to it. The sign O is applied by extrapolation to all that, in other frames of reference, might be called "ultimate unknowable reality," "absolute truth," "reality," "the thing-in-itself," the "infinite," the "unknown."

In psychoanalysis, when dealing with psychic reality or with the unconscious, we will apply the sign O to all that is unknowable about the patient, in other words, to his psychic reality, manifesting itself through multiple transformations.

The three types of transformation referred to so far are related to "knowing about O": they are transformations *from* O and can be included in the link K ("the ordinary view") and its counterpart –K ("the extraordinary view"). Bion adds transformations *in* O to these three models of transformation. It contrasts with the other three, in that it is related to change, growth, insight, and *becoming* O.

Bion says that reality cannot be known by definition, but it can "be." He calls this *becoming O*. Reality has to be "been": there should be a transitive verb *to be* expressly for use with the term *reality*.[4] The analyst is concerned with the reality of the patient's personality in such a way that he goes beyond "knowing about it," even though this knowing (K link) is an important part of the analytic process. Transformation *in* O is something like "being what one is," and this transformation is feared and therefore resisted.

The phenomenon of resistance can be understood as being opposed to the dangers implicit in becoming O. Insofar as becoming O is equivalent to "being oneself one's own truth," with its inherent responsibility, this "becoming" will be rejected because, among other things, it threatens the danger of megalomania. Nevertheless, only the interpretations which transform "knowing about something" into "becoming that something" (K→O), will produce change and mental growth.

Catastrophic Change: Evolution and Intuition

Transformations *in* O always have a disruptive character. In Bion's model this is described as *catastrophic change*.

This term links in constant conjunction events characterized by *violence, subversion of the system,* and *invariance* in the relation container-contained. The realizations corresponding to this constant conjunction may be found in different areas. If the container is the mind or the personality (with its characteristic structure at a given moment), and the contained is O, their interaction when becoming O will show all the characteristics described above, that is to say, violence, subversion of the existing system, and invariance in the process of transformation.

The neurotic personality faces problems derived from repressed infantile conflicts, which may become manifest in the analytic treatment as those transference phenomena implied, for example, by the theory of the Oedipus complex. In the theory of transformations, this area is covered by the term *rigid motion transformations* and in this context becoming O is "being" conscious of incestuous tendencies and the accompanying castration anxieties. The resistance the personality opposes to the transformation K → O includes the phenomenon of resistance classically described by Freud.

The area of the personality in which there is a predominance of projective transformations has partly been defined by the Kleinian theories of unconscious fantasies, part-object relations, and psychotic anxieties, thus corresponding to the theories of the paranoid-schizoid and depressive positions, with their characteristic defenses, especially pathological splitting and projective identification. In this context, becoming O is, for example, "being responsible" or "being greedy" or "being sadistic"; the resistances opposed to the transformation K→ O are related to these phenomena.

If the area we are dealing with corresponds to the transformations in hallucinosis, becoming O approximates to what is known as "being mad" or "being a murderer" or "being God." Realizations of this type belong to a state that has not been included in the theories mentioned above. What is needed is a new theoretical formulation that includes not only the realizations but also the mental and emotional states that represent them.

In these cases, catastrophic change has a peculiar quality

whose violence, together with a lack of container-mind to contain it, may produce an effect that transcends the frame of the psychoanalytic situation: it may expand explosively into other areas—the group, society, etc. Resistance to catastrophic change in the psychotic personality will be proportionately more violent and obstinate because its confrontation threatens a disruption that is also more intensely painful and violent.

In *Attention and Interpretation*,[5] Bion deals particularly with these problems. His approach is often centered on the analyst in the session, in the analytic experience, where he must undertake the difficult task of grasping the transformations from O, in order to interpret them in the hope of inducing the transformation $K \rightarrow O$ in the patient.

We can say that the reality we deal with as analysts, i.e. psychic reality, is infinite and has many facets. It is not originally an object of the senses. Bion proposes to use the verb *to intuit* to denote observation of psychic reality, in contrast to the methods of observation used in medicine (sight, touch, hearing, smell).

The psychoanalytic point of view, or, as Bion prefers to call it, the psychoanalytic *vertex,* is O, the unknown, new, and as yet not evolved. We assume it can develop to a point where our intuition can grasp it and make it coherent. The developments or evolutions of O are presented to the analyst's intuition and he must wait for such evolution to take place before he can formulate an interpretation.

The interpretation and the process that gives it shape, T (analyst) β and T (analyst) α, are given in terms derived from the senses, and can be classified as thoughts.

The process called *evolution* is the union, through a sudden intuition, of a mass of apparently disparate phenomena, thus givthem coherence and meaning. This process is analogous to that described by Poincare as the appearance of the "selected fact"[6] as a harmonizing factor in discovery, and it occurs—or should occur—in the mind of the analyst during the analytic session if he is in the right state of mind. This process can also be described in terms of the progression from the paranoid-schizoid position to the depressive position, or as the movement from being *patient* to being *secure*. The analyst who has not gone through these two phases of patience and security has not done the work that is required to give an interpretation. What is the adequate mental state for the intuitive grasp of the evolutions of O? Bion proposes the systematic avoidance of memory and desire, because they, with their roots in the senses, interfere with intuition and therefore with the possibility of contact with O in evolution.

This concept is very similar to that of free-floating attention and is easy to grasp if by "desire" one understands for instance "the desire that the session come to an end" or the "furor curandi," and by "memory," say, the tenacious memory of the latest psychoanalytic paper one has read as an aid in understanding the patient's material. It is obvious that these desires and memories interfere with the psycho-analytic contact with the patient. But Bion goes further in his proposal. He extends "memory" to all memory; he suggests that the analyst forget what he already knows about the patient and consider him a new patient in every session. This may place the analyst in a better condition to discover what he had previously ignored. Bion also extends "desire" to all desire, including the desire to understand, and admits the difficulty in achieving this stage and maintaining it. He justifies these requirements by the hypothesis that psychic reality is not sensuous and therefore our sensory equipment interferes with our capacity to grasp it. He points up the importance of the capacity to tolerate the suffering and frustration associated with "not knowing" and "not understanding." A lack of tolerance for this type of frustration can promptly lead the analyst to look for "fact and reason" to relieve him of his uncertainty. The interpretations derived from this precocious search for certainty, even though it may enhance knowledge, opposes discovery and the insight that is closely linked to becoming O.

The *language of achievement* derives from the possibility of tolerating half-doubts, half-mysteries and half-truths. It is the language that is at once a prelude to action and a type of action in itself. It is the language the analyst must achieve, and this language is related to the "capacity to forget, the ability to eschew desire and understanding"[7] when in contact with the patient during the unique and uncommunicable experience of each psychoanalytic session.

Notes

1. W. R. Bion, *Transformations,* Heinemann, London, 1965.

2. Ibid.

3. S. Freud, Remembering, repeating and working-through, S.E. 13.

4. W. R. Bion, op. cit.

5. W. R. Bion, *Attention and Interpretation,* Tavistock, London, 1970.

6. W. R. Bion, *Elements of Psycho-Analysis,* Heinemann, London, 1963, p. 39.

7. W. R. Bion, *Attention and Interpretation,* p. 51.

Chapter 5

TRANSFORMATION IN HALLUCINOSIS

Transformations in Hallucinosis • Space and Time in the Psychotic Area of the Personality • Mental Space in Hallucinosis

It is possible to approach the subject of hallucination from different angles. Its study has always aroused great interest and controversy, especially from the point of view of its origins, dynamics, and nature.

Freud,[1] in his theory of the psychic apparatus, explains that hallucinatory phenomena in the infant are the result of his tendency to satisfy a desire in the absence of the gratifying object. He calls this "hallucinatory realization of desires under the dominance of the pleasure principle."

When in normal development the infant's ego is faced with evidence that the hallucinatory realization of desires does not provide appropriate satisfaction, it will give up this method and replace it with others which are more realistic and use thoughts under the dominance of the reality principle. The persistence of this hallucinatory functioning of the psychic apparatus can be found in dream phenomena and in psychotic illnesses, among which Freud[2] places acute hallucinatory confusion (Meynert's "amentia"), which he partially explains as a regression to this primitive method of functioning.

Bion formulates the hypothesis that hallucinations are the product of evacuation of beta-elements and correspond therefore to a primitive mental level (row A of the grid). On the other hand, he places dream thoughts at a genetically higher level (characterized by the presence of alpha-elements) and postulates alpha-function as a prerequisite for the formulation of these dream thoughts (row C of the grid; see chapter 3). He conceptualizes hallucinatory phenomena as different from dreams, and attributes the former to the psychotic part of the personality.

The term *hallucination* comprises a series of phenomena which include manifest hallucinations (visual, auditory, tactile, etc.) and other phenomena not so obvious from the clinical point of view but genetically equivalent. "Fugative and evanescent" hallucinations and "invisible" hallucinations correspond, among others, to this type of phenomena.

These, together with manifest hallucinations and other phenomena, are included in a broader process that Bion called *transformations in hallucinosis.*

Transformations in Hallucinosis

Transformations in hallucinosis comprise a wide range of phenomena that belong to the psychotic part of the personality. We remind the reader that in all transformations (T) we take into account the following elements: O, the original experience (thing-in-itself); T-alpha (T α), (the process of transformation) where it is important to keep in mind the medium in which the transformation takes place and the rules used to carry it out; and T-beta (T β), (the end product or the point at which the transformation can be thought of as completed). We wish to emphasize the importance of the medium in which the transformations take place, since the end products of the process—which may be words or more complex statements such as formulated thoughts—can be evidence of either transformation in hallucinosis or transformation in thought.[3]

Bion assumes that this level of mental functioning exists in all human beings, even though it is no obstacle in the development of normal personality and may not manifest itself in behavior. Nevertheless, everyone on some occasions is afraid lest this mode of mental functioning become evident, especially in the context of psychoanalytic treatment.

Transformations in hallucinosis are correlated with a primitive "disaster" or "catastrophe," in which the emotional contents, things-in-themselves, beta-elements, have not found a container (mother with reverie) to contain and transform them. The "nameless dread" that is returned to the infant under these conditions, or "psychotic panic" as Bion also calls it, constitutes a mode of mental functioning in an area of infinite dimensions that cannot act as a container. In this state, the psychotic personality adopts defenses geared to avoid panic by evacuating the functions which would be capable of the experience.

The primitive emotional catastrophe, the O of hallucinosis, is transformed. The medium in which this transformation takes place is called the "psychotic area of the personality." The factors which operate in this transformation are envy associated with greed, which already participated in the original disaster but which is now proliferating as a "cancerous growth." The sense organs, usually used in perception, apprehension, and recognition of objects, become channels for evacuation of products or fragments formed during the process of transformation in hallucinosis. Muscles may also perform this evacuation function. Evacuation through the sense organs can be correlated to the presence of clinical evidence of visual, auditory, olfactory, or tactile hallucinations; evacuations through the muscles or through actions can be related to the clinical concept of acting out. Hallucinations, actions, or words used for evacuation can be seen as some of the T (patient) beta (Tp β) of the transformations in hallucinosis.

The processes (T α) of the transformations in hallucinosis described in more narrative terms (row C of the grid) can be expressed as follows: the person that uses this type of transformation believes that his "creations" are the result of his capacity to surround himself by a universe generated by himself to provide an "infallible" method of avoiding the pain of frustration. The patient "believes" that this method (transformation in hallucinosis) is superior to any other method that is proposed to him as help, especially the methods proposed by psychoanalysis or other therapy. This can also be formulated as "complete freedom from the restriction imposed by reality," because there is no such reality: the "reality" is the transformation in hallucinosis.

In other words, the patient in these conditions has to deny the existence of an external reality that restricts, oppresses and threatens him with the pain of frustration. Therefore, the only "reality" in which he "believes" is the "reality" generated by himself through the method of hallucinosis.

If we use the grid (see chapter 3) to characterize T beta (T β) of these transformations we shall see that they correspond to the category A (A1–A6), even though its formulation may have the appearance of other categories (rows, C, D, E, F, G, and H) when done through words or thoughts.

The capacity to tolerate the pain of frustration (formulated in other parts of this book as tolerance of catastrophic change) provides the basis for the development of the non-psychotic part of the personality and therefore for the development of transformations in thought or any other element with authentic representational qualities (music, painting, mathematics, etc.).

If we consider thoughts as a "statement of problems," these thoughts lead to a search for appropriate action, but if the personality is unable to tolerate the pain of frustration it will resort to transformations in hallucinosis and feel and develop all the processes described so far.

A system of hallucinosis is thus based on the intolerance of the absence of the object with the concomitant intolerance of the pain of frustration. The evacuation of beta-elements (hallucinations in the broad sense used by Bion) creates the "domain of the nonexistence" a mental world where what is nonexistent "exists" and therefore what does not exist is the painful suffering of frustration. The "gratification and freedom" provided by this system of hallucinosis is, from the point of view of an observer who uses transformations in thought, a "freedom" that is really an enclosure and a restriction. But from the point of view of the psychotic part of the personality, "freedom" resides in the immediacy of the result, without being "limited" by the creation of symbols, words, dreams, or other manifestations which have the quality of representing something.

Space and Time in the Psychotic Area of the Personality

Psychoanalytic theory often appears at a disadvantage in being formulated in such a descriptive way that the observational and theoretical levels seem confused, at the same level of abstraction. Theory may appear to be too concrete and therefore not suitable for generalization applicable to the many different emotional experiences that appear in a psychoanalytic treatment. On the other hand, it may appear too abstract. These problems become even more acute and urgent when we are faced with the task of studying concepts as complex as those related to development of a conception of time and space.

Bion deliberately proposes in this respect the use of abstract signs and manipulates them in the absence of the object of investigation (the analytic session). The use of grid categories is an important part of this method of investigation (see use of grid, chapter 3). (See Appendix § 5.)

Another proposal is the use of abstract signs such as (.) point and (—) line, to be employed as would a mathematician in his geometric and algebraic formulations. By employing such mathematical devices the analyst runs the danger of placing himself at too great a distance from the emotional situation with his patient for the sake of achieving freedom or thought. This method will be valid if one keeps this fact in mind, and the psychoanalyst will be able to maintain contact with the emotional background from which the abstract sign has been drawn. With this in mind, we shall now focus on these two signs: the point (.) and the line (—). Both must be considered as representing two series of ideas.

In the first, the point (.) and the line (—) represent a constant conjunction; they function as a definitory hypothesis and their evolution will depend on the degree to which the negative aspect of the definitory hypothesis is tolerated (in the same way that to indicate what "is" indicates also that something "is not"; the symbol represents what "is" but "is not" what is symbolized). Seen in this way, the point and the line indicate objects, and all the considerations about object relations developed by Melanie Klein apply to them. In the second series of ideas, the point (.) and the line (—) represent time and space that infuse objects and object relations. In this case, (.) and (—) can symbolically express the "position the object occupies in space and in time" as a more elaborate response of the non-psychotic part of the personality to the absence of the object.

Instead, the psychotic part of the personality does not tolerate such absence and "establishes" space as a presence. Through a transformation in hallucinosis it changes the "now-is-not" temporal sequence and the "here-is-not" spatial sequence into "now-is-here."

The transformation in hallucinosis is a particular form of

functioning of the psychotic area of the personality and creates a space occupied by nonexistent objects, sometimes by manifest hallucinations and at other times by equivalent phenomena (evanescent hallucinations, invisible hallucinations).

This "occupied" space is represented by the sign minus point –(.) and minus line –(—). They represent methods of substitution for a non-occupied space-time. Since this condition is not tolerated by the psychotic part of the personality, it attacks with envy and greed this unoccupied state of space-time and the concepts and symbols which represent them, stripping them of their representational function.

Mental Space in Hallucinosis

The model of the psychic apparatus described by Freud[4] illustrated in his diagram of Ego, Superego, and Id, is based on a realization of a physical aspect. This model has shown its usefulness in explaining many events but is inadequate for investigating patients with disturbances in their orientation to time and space. To approach the understanding of these disturbances, the model used for investigation must be one in which the realization approximates to the model used by the patient.

Mental space, as postulated by Bion, is a thing-in-itself and therefore unknowable.

Mental space can be represented by thoughts, words, etc., but this inevitably limits it. The Kleinian theory of projective identification is formulated in terms derived from a realization of the ordinary area of three-dimensional space; these formulations depend on a visual image of a space that contains all sorts of objects. It is into such a space that a person is conceived to project the split-off parts of his personality. However, analytic work with seriously dis-

turbed patients has led Bion to attempt a more rigorous
formulation of mental space, for he considers that in certain
types of patients the notions of space and time obey the
realization of psychotic fantasies based on a psychic reality
which does not derive its form from physical reality.

The emotional experience called *psychotic panic,* O of the
transformation in hallucinosis, is an experience that can be
conceived as a failure of alpha-function to form a container
(♀) that will "contain" violent emotions. The incapacity to
form a contained (♂) that can tolerate waiting for a
container (♀), together with the failure to form a constant
conjunction associated with a selected fact (Ps→D operation) is conducive to the relation ♀ ♂ not being established
or to the establishment of a relation – ♀ ♂ . There is a
failure of realistic projective identification and what occurs
instead is an "explosive projection," which is an experience
in a "mental space" which has nothing to restrict it. This
emotional experience causes space to be felt to be of such
immensity that it cannot be represented even by astronomi-
cal space. The relation between the container and the
contained is so explosive and devastating that it does not
allow anything to represent it. It does not accept the
formation of symbols.

Bion provides a medical-biological model for the
understanding of the emotional experience of the psychotic
mental space. He suggests it can be compared to surgical
shock where the dilation of the capillaries so increases the
space in which blood circulates that the patient in effect
bleeds to death in his own tissues.

The mental space generated by the psychotic part of the
personality is so vast compared with habitual three-
dimensional space that the patient feels his emotions getting
lost in an infinite vacuum, like the blood in the medical
model. Words, images, and ideas of these patients are
remnants, debris, or fragments floating in a space without
limits (mental space of hallucinosis). Alternatively, they
may be grouped together in an attempt at synthesis, by

forming conglomerates. They are evacuated as beta-elements or bizarre objects that mark the "place where the object *should be.*"

To summarize, Bion proposes a description in which (.) and (—), ♀ ♂ , are attacked by the psychotic part of the personality with violent devastating emotions, among which we mentioned the association of envy and greed as being particularly destructive; this results in a spoiling force that strips the incipient formation of concepts of space and time of their meaning.

The development of a non-psychotic concept of space and time stems from the establishment of a constant conjunction of facts of experience in relation to the presence and absence of the object. This conjunction is impregnated with tolerable emotions and this allows us to consider it as a definitory hypothesis (.) and (—), which, in a non-saturated form, retains the possibility of being used as a preconception. New emotional experiences will lead to formulations and concepts that are increasingly complex, with a tolerance toward the presence-absence, "now" and "not now," and "here" and "not here." This leads to growth conceived as evolution.

Point (.) and line (—) are signs which (as definitory hypotheses) can represent but not substitute. They function as preconceptions that in successive negative realizations (frustration, absence of the object) will facilitate with increasing frequency the construction of symbols in the area of thought and in the area of action, setting the basis for words to become a prelude to action and not a substitute for it. Some examples will illustrate these concepts: a patient says repeatedly that he is "wasting time". This formulation will have a very different interpretation if we can understand that it is not a verbal transformation but a concrete and actual event for the psychotic part of the personality. In a similar way, words like *yesterday, later,* or *some years ago* may not be representations but residues of destructive dispersing attacks on time. In order to detect this in the patient's material the observer should be able to relinquish partially the accustomed mode of transforming and to approach an understanding of the patient's mode of transformation. Another example: in the course of his analysis a patient makes references to a certain event, but these references, separated by months or even years, can hardly be recognized by an observer as dispersed fragments of an attacked emotional experience. Nevertheless, they are for the psychotic part of the personality a "stretched" present, a moment in time that also measure the concrete distance between the dispersed fragments. The understanding of acting out in relation to an infinite and dispersed "mental space" provides a new perspective for the understanding of problems related to this "mental space."

Transformation in hallucinosis implies the realization of transformations from O, thing-in-itself, in a context different from that of verbal or symbolic transformation. The point (.) and the line (—) are not tolerated because of an envious attack on the incipient concept of space and time that strips them of their representative qualities leaving only things-in-themselves, beta-elements, evacuations. The point (.) become minus point –(.), the line (—) becomes minus line –(—), and the space a "non-space" that has the threatening characteristics with which it was invested.

Notes

1. S. Freud, The interpretation of dreams, S.E. 5.

2. S. Freud, A metapsychological supplement to the theory of dreams, S.E. 14.

3. Transformations in thought are rigid transformations that can be represented by words and therefore verbalized.

4. S. Freud, The ego and the id, S.E. 19.

Chapter 6

KNOWLEDGE

L, H and K links • Myths as Models of the K link • The Psychoanalytic Object • Vertices, Correlation and Confrontation • Truth, Falsity and Lies

Bion's theory of thought and thinking is also a theory about knowing, about learning from experience and its disturbances. He develops concepts about the origin and acquisition of knowledge as well as some formulations about "psychoanalytic knowledge." He takes into account the evolution of the individual's knowledge about himself and others, the learning relationships of the individual in the group, and those of one group with other groups.

The theory of knowledge which can be discerned in Bion's work is a theory that assumes that all knowledge has its origins in primitive emotional experiences related to the absence of the object. Characteristics that are inherent in this emotional experience sometimes intervene in an attenuated form in the later experiences of discovery, learning, and formulation of new ideas in any field, whether scientific, esthetic, psychoanalytic, or whatever. He proposes to discover similar configurations in very dissimilar experiences, i.e. to point out invariants or equivalent structures every time the individual, group, or society are faced with a problem of knowledge.

Bion assumes that the ultimate reality of the object is unknowable in the Kantian sense of the term. The object of knowledge in psychoanalysis is one's own or another person's psychic reality. Investigation of it poses various problems. One of the main problems is related to the fact that this object of knowledge, psychic reality, is not an object in the physical sense. The basic emotions the psychoanalyst deals with—anxiety, love, fear, hate—cannot be apprehended with the sense organs (they cannot be touched, heard, or seen), but verbal and bodily transformations of them can be discriminated. The problem posed by psychoanalytic experience is, in a sense, the lack of an adequate terminology to describe such events and resembles the problem that Aristotle solved by supposing that mathematics dealt with mathematical objects.

Bion suggests that it is convenient to assume that the psychoanalyst deals with *psychoanalytic objects*.[1] The psychoanalyst tries to detect them in the course of psychoanalytic treatment and through successive abstractions and transformations he attempts to find a way of communicating the nature of these objects.

This process of intuition, abstraction, and transformation is similar in some of its characteristics to the process of discovery and abstraction that Bion assumes takes place in the infant's mind during development. Thanks to his alphafunction, the infant deduces from his first emotional experiences the models and concepts he will use as hypotheses in his contact with internal and external reality. From constant evolutive interplay his conceptions, concepts, vocabulary, and language will arise, allowing all possible developments and uses.

L, H and K Links

During this developmental process the personality comes across the problem of bearing the frustration inherent in the experience called K link.

The word *link* describes the emotional experience that is ever present when two people or two parts of a person are related to each other. Bion selects three of these emotions—Love (L), Hate (H), and Knowledge (K)—as intrinsic to the link between two objects, as the requisite for the existence of a relationship.

The sign K, derived from the first letter of the word *knowledge,* is used to refer to the link between a subject which tries to know an object, and an object which can be known. The K link represents an active link and refers to an emotional experience which has a particular shade, different from that represented by the L link and the H link. This particular emotional shade is expressed by the painful feeling which can be discerned in the question "How can X (the subject) know anything?"; it can be formulated as the pain or frustration inherent in knowledge.

The K link can typify the individual who tries to know the truth about himself through introspection. It also characterizes the psychoanalytic relationship between an analyst and a patient. Knowing the truth about oneself is a function of the personality. Bion suggests that Freud[2] implicitly attributed this function to consciousness when he defined it as "the sense organ for the perception of psychical qualities." The development of this function of the personality is achieved through successive and multiple emotional experiences where the operations Ps↔D and ♀ ♂ intervene (chapter 3). This function of perceiving psychic qualities is basically related to the knowledge of psychic reality and is called by Bion *the psychoanalytic function of the personality.* This function exists from the beginning of life and is developed by the psychoanalytic method.

Analogous to the preconception, the K link refers to an expectation of knowing something which has not as yet been realized. Using the container-contained model (♀ ♂), it suggests that a relationship between the two exists on an emotional background of tolerated doubt.

The attitude called *knowing* is the activity through which the subject becomes aware of the emotional experience and can abstract from it a formulation which adequately represents this experience. The process of abstraction is essential to the emotional experience of the K link, because the abstracted elements can be used for learning from experience and for understanding.

This process is carried out by the relation between container and contained (♀ ♂) and the dynamic interaction between the paranoid-schizoid position and the depressive position (Ps↔D). The latter operation describes processes of integration and disintegration similar to what Poincaré described as the discovery of the selected fact.

It is necessary to distinguish between the "possession of knowledge" as the result of a *modification* of pain in the K link (in which case the knowledge acquired will be employed for further discoveries) and the "possession of knowledge" that is used to evade the painful experience. The latter can be found to predominate in the omniscient part of the personality. The establishment of a K link, and therefore of learning through emotional experience, is precluded.

This evasion of pain can be at the service of an activity called "–K link" (minus K), an emotional state in which all the factors suggested for K are reversed. The emotional factors in –K are envy and greed, and in terms of a container-contained they constitute a relation which is mutually spoiling and destructive, where meaning and emotion are actively denuded of vitality and sense so that discovery and development become impossible. The –K link substitutes morality for scientific thought. There will be no function in this approach for discriminating between true and false, between thing-in-itself and representation. In describing this link, Bion is defining the domain of the psychotic personality or the psychotic part of the personality. This link can also be called parasitic and takes place between two objects which relate to one another in a manner that will produce a third one destructive for all three.

Myths as Models of the K Link

Myths have been a source of knowledge for very diverse disciplines (see Appendix § 6). Psychoanalysis has found in the Oedipus myth an illumination of the details of sexual development, as Freud demonstrated through his use of the theory of the Oedipus complex. Investigation of the oedipal situation in its multiple and changing realizations has proved valuable for promoting the development of patients in analytic treatment; it also nurtured the development of psychoanalytic theory, as for instance the formulation of the early stages of the Oedipus complex. Psychoanalytic discoveries in turn allowed for a richer understanding of myths. Love, hate, sex, and jealousy (L and H links) play a predominant role in all these studies.

Bion proposes, by way of example, to approach the Oedipus myth by searching for elements related to the K link, that is to say, to the problem of knowledge, considering this at least as basic in the human being as the L and H links. From this angle he finds a common underlying structure related to the K link in three very different narrative myths: the Garden of Eden, Oedipus, and the Tower of Babel.

The common elements to be found in these three myths are an omniscient and omnipotent god, a model for mental growth through an attitude of curiosity and challenge, and punishment related to the prohibition against curiosity and the search for truth. In the Eden myth the challenge consists of eating the forbidden apple from the Tree of Knowledge, an act punished by expulsion from earthly paradise. Oedipus' curiosity about himself is represented by the riddle of the Sphinx. The challenge resides in the arrogant and obstinate manner in which Oedipus carries out his investigation, despite the warnings of Tiresias, and the punishment consists of blindness and exile. In the Babel myth curiosity and thirst for knowledge (to reach Heaven) meet the challenge by construction of a tower, and a city is punished by the confusion of languages and destruction of the capacity to communicate. Significantly, in all three myths curiosity has the quality of being a sin. The models for mental growth are represented by the Tree of Knowledge, the riddle of the Sphinx and the Tower of Babel.

The underlying configuration of these myths is identical in relation to "knowing." Stimulated curiosity searches for knowledge; intolerance to pain and fear of the unknown stimulate actions and these actions tend to avoid, cancel out, or neutralize the search and the curiosity. Column 2 of the grid (see chapter 3) allows us to locate the phenomenon of resistance which opposes the discovery of new truths. Myths give a narrative version of the problem; each of the three describes the drama of the relationship of the individual to the group with respect to the search for self-knowledge.

Bion suggests that the Oedipus myth is part of a primitive apparatus which operates as a preconception in the infant's mind. This preconception refers to the parental couple and will be realized through contact with real or substitute parents. The "Oedipal myth–preconception" is a precursor of knowledge of psychic reality. Therefore Bion postulates the "private Oedipus myth" formed by alpha-elements and suggests that it is an essential part of the learning apparatus in the early stages of the child's development. This private Oedipus myth–preconception is thus a factor in the psychoanalytic function of the personality.

This private myth, which allows the infant to understand his relation with the parental couple, can suffer destructive attacks coming from envy, greed, and sadism, which are constitutionally present. The consequences of the destructive attack are fragmentation and dispersion of this preconception, obstructing the evolution of the intuitive dimension of an apparatus for learning from experience. In consequence the development of the psychoanalytic function of the personality will be impaired.

The Psychoanalytic Object

Psychoanalysis has tried to delimit its object of study, and the psychoanalytic developments arrived at are evidence that this has, to a certain extent, been achieved. The difficulties inherent in the communication of experiences among analysts show, nevertheless, that there is a need for a stricter limitation of the nature of the object of study.

The characteristics of that object of study which is linked to psychic reality or to unconscious fantasies, and which Bion proposes to call the "psychoanalytic object," are its non-sensorial quality and the possibility of "growing," "decreasing," "being," and "becoming." These terms, however, evoke associations inappropriate to the description of the psychoanalytic object. To lessen this difficulty Bion suggests the use of an abstraction-formula that allows a smaller range of associations. The formula he proposes is: $\pm$ Y (μ) (ξ) (ψ).

The letter Y refers to the mental growth factor and can be negative or positive $(\pm)$. (Mu) (μ) represents the character of the personality. (Epsilon) (ξ) is the non-saturated element of the preconception, ψ (psi).

Psychoanalytic theory assumes a genetic continuity which starts in a primitive emotional experience, and through development produces a structure. The psychoanalyst undertakes to reveal and describe through his interpretations the "here and now" of the session with its primitive emotional happenings and their derivatives. What is the psychoanalytic object of any session? What does the analyst try to reveal with his interpretation? The analyst is assuming the existence of an object which manifests itself through associations, gestures, and emotions of the patient in contact with himself. If we apply Bion's formula, we shall find that this object has elements or factors which are part of the innate character of the patient's personality (μ), with the availability (ξ) of his preconception (ψ)—expectation that can be saturated to a greater or lesser degree in the experience-realization of the analytic session. The discernible psychoanalytic object will also have a direction which can be characterized as progression or regression, or in other terms, as growth or decrease ($\pm Y$).

The psychoanalytic object, which we have described as appearing in the patient's material in the psychoanalytic session, has its genetic history in the development of thought in the individual. It is therefore possible to describe this psychoanalytic object in its earliest stages, by using the model of the relation between the infant and the breast, as explained in chapter 3; the constituting elements can be represented by the formula. In this formula, ψ (ξ) represents the non-saturated expectation-preconception of the breast, with its innate character mu (ψ) which can develop in different forms ($\pm Y$) according to the vicissitudes described in chapter 3. This psychoanalytic object, with its constitutive elements, forms part of a function related to the knowledge of psychic reality, which Bion calls the psychoanalytic function of the personality.

In the analytic situation, the analyst in a K link with the patient abstracts an interpretation from the psychoanalytic object. From his emotional experience when in contact with the patient, he determines the values of μ (mu) and ξ (epsilon); the formulation of the interpretation will include these emotional elements in a new dimension (the mythic dimension), the model he has created in his mind for the situation he wishes to interpret. Insofar as the interpretation clarifies this psychoanalytic object, it will acquire dimensions in the sense of myth, of meaning, and of theory.

The psychoanalytic object has been apprehended through what we called the "state of discovery," where intuition is a most important factor. The method the analyst can use to encourage intuition is expressed in the attitude proposed by Bion of "no memory, no desire, no understanding." This state facilitates psychoanalytic interpretation. Once interpreted, the psychoanalytic object will have changed. Every new interpretation must arise from a similar process of abstraction, keeping in mind the new emotional experience and the multiple facets of psychic reality.

Vertices, Correlation and Confrontation

The concept of *vertex* refers to the "point of view," "angle," or "perspective" from which one tries first to understand and then to communicate a particular experience, as for instance the psychoanalytic. This experience can be described in many ways; clarification of vertex can help to communicate precisely and clearly. (See Appendix § 7.)

Each of the members of the analtyic couple, analyst and patient, will have his own vertex in relation to the experience they share. These vertices must keep a useful distance from one another, neither too near nor too distant. When this useful distance is achieved, the possibility will arise of a correlation and a confrontation between these vertices, providing a binocular view of the problem at hand. If the distance is minimal, the analyst's vertex will not differ from that of the patient, and the attempt to detect and clarify the psychoanalytic object will fail. The same happens if the points of view are too distant, rendering correlation between them impossible.

The possibility of correlating two different vertices occurs not only between two personalities but also within one personality, giving place to states of confusion or to binocular vision, depending on the distance between them.

Vertices or perspectives can be of very diverse sorts. We can mention, for instance, the social, political, educational, financial, scientific, philosophical, moral, religious, sexual, superego, paternal, false, true, and psychoanalytic vertices. Most of Bion's conceptualizations attempt to characterize and specify the psychoanalytic vertex.

Difficulty in the communication between analysts may arise for different reasons. The differences of vertices can be an important factor in this, despite apparent similarity in the theories and conceptual schemes employed. Two psychoanalysts belonging to different psychoanalytic schools can communicate and understand each other if they share a psychoanalytic vertex, even though their theories and conceptual schemes may differ.

Truth, Falsehood and Lies

The complexity of the problems investigated by Bion concerning truth, falsehood, and lies makes their formulation difficult. Bion suggests that, once formulated, all thoughts are false if compared with the "true" fact they formulate. What varies is the degree of falsification, and here it would be necessary to differentiate truth from lie or rather lie from truth. These concepts are of enormous importance for the psychoanalyst, who is often struggling both with patients who lie and with the liar in himself.

Truth is essential for mental growth. Without truth the psychic apparatus does not develop and dies of starvation. A mother with *reverie* senses the truth in the baby's feelings and returns them to her child in a tolerable form. The baby discovers that his mother is a whole object and this discovery of correlation and confrontation is a fundamental milestone in his mental evolution, in the acquisition of language, and in the possibility of communicating. Melanie Klein showed how interrelated were the depressive position and symbolization. When psychoanalytic interpretations clarify some aspect of psychic reality—the analytic object—they provide partial truths which foster development and mental growth in the patient.

It is possible to refer to the absolute truth as a "thought without a thinker." The thought which has not yet been thought could be considered as a contained which has not found a container. It is an idea without shape, unarticulated as evidence of "something." It coexists with the thinker without as yet coming in contact with him. An example of this situation is infantile sexuality, which undoubtedly existed before Freud made it obvious and formulated it as a theory. Psychoanalysts are used to living with certain "truths" of their patients without discovering them. We already referred to the mental state that is more conducive to the discovery of this reality or truth. We shall come back to this point later.

The relation between thinker and "thought" may be commensal, symbiotic, or parasitic. In the first case, the *commensal* state between the new idea and the thinker, they do not influence each other. This may change when the idea and the thinker meet in a moment of mutual evolution. When this happens, a catastrophic change takes place. From this catastrophic change there then emerges a *symbiotic* relation in which thought and thinker grow and develop to their mutual benefit. Formulated thoughts emerge that will be false because they are included in the relation container-contained in K, which means that they are false because, compared with the original truth, they contain a restriction. This truth, which can only have "been," is apprehended by intuition and undergoes both rigid and projective transformations, which give rise to representations, symbols, new concepts, or formulae.

If the relation between thought and thinker is *parasitic,* if the link is −K, the result of the intersection will be in some cases the proliferation of lies as a barrier against truth. Bion considers it necessary to have a thinker in order to produce a lie; whereas true thought does not require the prior existence of a thinker. In the parasitic relationship, thought and thinker destroy each other with loss of vitality and meaning. Liars, in whom thoughts have proliferated almost without limit, require truths; but when these are included in the parasitic relationship they are again denuded of their essential quality and transformed into lies. It is essential that the psychoanalyst detect his patient's lies, and his own.

At the same time it seems that the human being's capacity to tolerate truths about himself is fragile; truth is a permanent source of pain and the wish for knowledge can never be satisfied or completed; therefore the tendency to evasive action is great and the mind is always prepared to create lies to oppose this pain.

We transcribe here a fable that Bion includes in *Attention and Interpretation*[3] to show the liar's point of view or vertex vis à vis the scientific approach in which truth assumes a predominant role.

"The liars showed courage and resolution in their opposition to the scientists who with their pernicious doctrines bid fair to strip every shred of self-deception from their dupes leaving them without any of the natural protection necessary for the preservation of their mental health against the impact of truth. Some, knowing full well the risks that they ran, nevertheless laid down their lives in affirmations of lies so that the weak and doubtful would be convinced by the ardor of their conviction of the truth of even the most preposterous statements. It is not too much to say that the human race owes its salvation to that small band of gifted liars who were prepared even in the face of indubitable facts to maintain the truth of their falsehoods. Even death was denied and the most ingenious arguments were educed to support obviously ridiculous statements that the dead lived on in bliss. These martyrs to untruth were often of humble origin whose very names have perished. But for them and the witness borne by their obvious sincerity the sanity of the race must have perished under the load placed on it. By laying down their lives they carry the morals of the world on their shoulders. Their lives and the lives of their followers were devoted to the elaboration of systems of great intricacy and beauty in which the logical structure was preserved by the exercise of a powerful intellect and faultless reasoning. By contrast the feeble processes by which the scientists again and again attempted to support their hypotheses made it easy for the liars to show the hollowness of the pretensions of the upstarts and thus to delay, if not to prevent, the spread of doctrines whose effect could only have been to induce a sense of helplessness and unimportance in the liars and their beneficiaries."

Notes

1. The term *psychoanalytic object* is not related to the word *object* as used in psychoanalytic literature. Here it means an "object of knowledge."
2. S. Freud, The interpretation of dreams, S.E. 5.
3. W. R. Bion, *Attention and Interpretation,* pp. 100–101.

Chapter 7

REFLECTIONS ON THE PRACTICE OF PSYCHOANALYSIS

The title of this chapter[1] may awaken doubts in the reader's mind. Who is to be the subject of the discussion? Are we referring to Bion and his personal way of approaching the practice of psychoanalysis? Or do we wish to put forward our own conclusions and understanding of Bion's ideas in their application to the field of clinical psychoanalysis?

Both go together in all likelihood. In the development of the concepts we shall be putting forward, we can show the end-product, T (authors of this book) β, of the process of transformation we made from studying his books, from listening to his lectures, seminars, and supervisions and from our dialogue with him, when discussing certain specific problems.

We want to start by pointing out one of the attitudes we found most significant in his approach to the subject. His conviction that analysis is a dynamic and lively interchange between two people who listen and talk to each other in a particular way, and not merely an intellectual and sophisticated adaptation between a "psychoanalyst" and a "patient," gives primary importance to the clinical experience. Bion considers that stereotypes, the therapist's fantasies of omnipotence, and this tendency to cling to theoretical a priori knowledge are the analyst's chief reactions in the face of the something new and unknown that appears in every analytic session.

According to Bion the evaluation and development of psychoanalytic practice can be hindered by the deficiency or absence of a precise elaboration of the elements which constitute psychoanalysis. These elements combine in a particular way at every moment of the clinical experience, and provide a specificity that characterizes each clinical manifestation, making it different from any other.

In putting forward these considerations, we want to underline two important aspects: in the first place, the idea that these elements can combine in such a way as to represent all psychoanalytic situations as well as all analytic theories; second, the possibility that the elements considered essential can be detected, observed, and recognized by their secondary qualities (in the Kantian sense of the term) during the psychoanalytic experience.

Here we meet Bion essentially as an analyst, stimulating us to approach the clinical phenomena of analysis in full possession of our observational capacity; this can be improved with the use of certain special resources that will avoid the interferences that can obscure the observation, as we will see later. It also forms the basis of what is a true *observational theory of psychoanalytic practice,* a theory in which the elements of psychoanalysis can also be isolated.

On the other hand, Bion confronts us with a transcendental problem when he asks what the emotional experience of a particular analytic session depends on; for it to be considered psychoanalysis and nothing else? In other words, which of the constituent elements determine the psychoanalytic specificity of such an experience? He especially underlines, among its emotional peculiarities, the atmosphere of deprivation, isolation, and loneliness in which both participants must find themselves. *Deprivation* must necessarily result from the analyst's resistance to any impulse to gratify his patient's or his own desires, as well as from the patient's resistance to his tendency to act. Both analyst and patient suffer a sense of *isolation* because certain types of responsibility cannot be shared or delegated, for instance, that belonging to the circumstances which have led the patient to analysis and to the analyst's decision to take the patient in analysis. The decision to formulate an interpretation, with the subsequent consequences, cannot be shared or delegated either. *Loneliness* appears when, in dealing with the object of scrutiny—the patient's psychic reality—the patient feels abandoned as far as the satisfaction of his most primitive physical and emotional needs are concerned. The analyst similarly experiences loneliness, as if he were "cutting himself off from the source or base on which he depends for his existence"; this means that he feels he must part from those external and internal objects that make up his basic links, activities, and needs. This painful feeling is related to introspection. (See Appendix § 8.)

The peculiarity of an analytic session also resides in the use the analyst makes of all the material refering to the transference situation. Transference can be found in all those aspects of a patient's behavior which reveal his knowledge of the presence of an object that is not himself. This object can be the person of the analyst, his greeting or no greeting, any of the furniture, or a reference to the weather.

Bion points out that analysis should evolve in such a way as to create the conditions which will allow the analyst to perceive through his "premonitions" the imminent contents of preconceptions. He emphasizes the importance of the analyst's being able to intuit the emotion before it becomes "painfully obvious" to the analysand. In this case, the element to be investigated is a precursor of the emotion. One of the aims of psychoanalytic intuition is to avoid unnecessary pain.

Nevertheless, before we proceed, we have to establish here an important differentiation. We have mentioned *unnecessary pain,* to differentiate it from the inevitable which must occur in any analysis. The analytic treatment offers the necessary conditions for the analysand to obtain knowledge about himself. But the attempt to know implies a painful feeling which is inherent in the emotional experience of knowledge. In any case, pain cannot be absent from the individual's personality. If the analyst does not detect this pain he will be unable to modify it, and will fail to fulfill one of his main functions. Progress in an analysis is inseparable from the need to tolerate the pain concomitants of mental growth. As in medicine, the disappearance of the capacity for pain would be disastrous. The patient may tend to evade pain before modifying it, but a very strong evasion endangers his contact with reality.

Unlike the situation in medical practice, where the illness may be recognized exclusively by the physician, such recognition must be carried out in psychoanalysis by two people: the analyst and the patient. In order to carry out his function, the physician depends a great deal on his sensory experience, trying to see, touch, and hear. The analyst, on the other hand, is not dependent primarily on his sensory experience; for instance, the anxiety he will have to detect has no shape, color, sound, or smell, and he will have to rely as much on his intuition as on the observations which can be registered by his sense organs.

Psychoanalysis must be considered a term which binds a constant conjunction, even though it is difficult to be concise about the constituents of this constant conjunction. The psychoanalytic situation stimulates basic and primitive feelings in both the analysand and the analyst. This is the reason why such emotions as love, hate, and fear may become acute to the point where they may become unbearable to the analytic couple. This is the price that must be paid for the transformation of an activity *about* psychoanalysis into another activity that *is* psychoanalysis. Bion points out that criticizing a psychoanalytic task as "non-scientific" would be as absurd as criticizing it because it is "not religious" or "not artistic" (see Appendix § 9). In any case, the only useful critical formulation would be, "It is not psychoanalysis."

On the other hand Bion maintains that the domain of the personality is so vast that it cannot be totally investigated. It cannot, therefore, be said that an analysis has been "completed." No matter how long a psychoanalytic treatment lasts, it always represents the beginning of an investigation which stimulates growth in the area being investigated: the knowledge of psychic reality. When a person has finished his analysis his knowledge about himself is greater than when he started, but if we observe the relation between what he knows about himself and his psychic reality, which has also been growing during the psychoanalytic process, the relative proportion of his knowledge is probably smaller. Therefore, Bion advises us not to waste time on what has already been discovered but to focus mainly on what is yet to be known.

Psychoanalytic treatment in Bion's view consists of a task in which there is a confrontation of the adult and infantile aspects of the patient. It is of interest to know the patient's internal world and his psychopathology, but also the real external events in which he takes part.

It will always be useful to get the patient to talk about the external event which manifestly or latently worries him, to avoid the risk of denying the importance of external reality and of the anxieties and depressions related to it. One will in this way obtain more information. The external event will be used to draw attention to the unconscious elements that contribute to the painful nature of these experiences. The external event throws light on the neurosis and is at the same time illuminated by it: the two interact.

Even though the practice of psychoanalysis predominantly tends to investigate the unconscious of the analysand, it develops on the basis of the conscious participation of both components of the analytic couple. It is convenient not to overlook the fact that in the neurotic patient the conscious elements have the same value as the unconscious ones. Both have to be correlated, underlined, and seen in their real meaning within the context of the analytic process in order to provide a binocular vision.

On the other hand, the psychotic patient is aware of things a less disturbed patient would repress. In this case the purpose of analysis may be to help the patient form a "contact barrier" that will allow him to differentiate his conscious from his unconscious experiences and therefore to dream, repress, forget, etc.

The importance Bion attributes to the conscious cooperation and participation of the patient is shown in some of his comments about the first interview. If, for example, a patient says: "Well, I have come because my father, or my mother, told me to or because my wife says I must have treatment," one could ask: "But do you do everything your wife says? Do you always obey your parents? And if not, why is this an exception?" It will be useful to pay attention to the type of response from the patient, because if he disclaims responsibility from the beginning it will not make a favorable starting point for the analysis.

The awareness of illness can also be evaluated when considering the problem of fees and what it means for the patient beyond its realistic aspect. So, for example, he can say "that does not bother me," denying any importance to the problem, or "I am sorry but I have no time," or "I haven't enough money to pay that fee," whatever the amount might be. What the patient means is that he can afford a neurosis, but that he, like his society, has no idea of the tremendous price he pays for the "privilege" of having it. On the other hand, other individuals have reached a point at which they feel that the state of their mind is not an advantage but a burden, and seek help from analysis.

Bion does not exclude the possibility of formulating interpretations in the first interview, to provide the patient with the chance of finding out what kind of person the analyst is, and what kind of treatment he is being offered.

What is important in each case is to assess the capacity of the patient to establish correlations, and the capacity of the analyst to tolerate this particular patient.

Once psychoanalytic treatment has started, it is assumed that interpretations genuinely reflect what happens in the dynamic field of the two-person relationship. The more purposeful they are, the quicker the patient will become a unique and specific personality. Psychoanalytic interpretations can be considered the models the analyst has about the theories the patient has about his analyst and about psychoanalysis.

It will be useful to formulate interpretations in such a way as not to close the discussion or the subject that is being dealt with, that is to say, as not to saturate the possibilities of development. This will especially be achieved when interpretations "throw more light than heat" so that the patient can tolerate the suffering produced by the experience of *insight* when faced with feared or rejected situations. Walpole's concept of serendipity could be applied to interpretations. This type of discovery arises when one stumbles on things which throw light on other things. This allows an understanding of and knowledge about them which was hitherto absent.

The patient's associations and the analyst's interpretations are ineffable. The analytic session is a type of experience that can be shared only by the analysand and his analyst, and cannot be transmitted in its essence to a third person. This is why communication of a recorded session, be it for supervision or in a scientific paper, will inevitably be imperfect. The relation between the analytic couple is of such a nature that no mental event in one can be said to be understood without reference to the state of mind of the other.

There will always be new situations in the course of the analytic session. If something has been interpreted which later reappears, it will now be in a new context different from the previous one. The patient may, for example, refer to the "same depression" or the "same phobia" in order to avoid the painful realization of something new and unknown in his psychic reality.

It is necessary to remain alert to the appearance of new aspects of the material in order not to waste the session, as it is our only opportunity to be with the patient. The fifty minutes of the session are much too valuable to be wasted in repeating what is already known.

It would also be useful to tolerate the uncertainty and anxiety of not knowing, the incoherence of the material, and the lack of understanding, until a way of seeing it coherently can be found and new relations can be discovered among its elements. Applying Melanie Klein's concepts, this would mean to move from the "paranoid-schizoid position" to the "depressive position." But Bion prefers to apply these terms to what happens to the analysand. Insofar as the analyst is concerned he uses the term *patience* to refer to a mental state which corresponds to the paranoid-schizoid position (because he must tolerate frustration and suffering and be "patient" while confronting "scattered facts" without feelings of persecution); he proposes the term *security* for the mental state experienced after the discovery of the "selected fact"—a state of less anxiety and of freedom from dangers. Bion considers the interpretations which appear after passing through these two emotional phases the only indicators of adequate analytic work.

For Bion, psychoanalytic interpretations are the result of a series of transformations which stem from a certain original experience between analyst and patient, and which reveal the invariants of such experience.

The psychoanalytic experience implies both a knowledge about oneself and being oneself. The interpretations which make the transition from "knowing about" psychic reality (transformations in K) to "becoming" each one of the emotions which are part of psychic reality (transformations in O) are feared and arouse resistance. For Bion, this passage from K to O (from knowing O to becoming O) is fundamental for mental growth.

Becoming O implies assuming responsibility for one's own feelings whatever their nature (responsibility for murderous feelings, feelings of "madness," incestuous feelings, feelings of being a genius, etc.). When transformations in K threaten appearance of transformations in O, the fear of "psychological turbulence" of catastrophic change arises. A resistance to change from K to O takes place out of fear of painful suffering associated with insight.

Another reason for resistance to the transformation of becoming O is that instead of assuming the responsibility for the representation of the feared feeling, the analyst is actually afraid he will become the thing he most fears: "mad," "a murderer," "incestuous," "a genius," etc. These fears include the danger of megalomania.

The analyst will, to a certain extent, be able to anticipate that a specific interpretation may succeed in becoming O, because of his own difficulty and doubt in formulating it due to the strong resistance he anticipates it will provoke in the analysand.

We would now like to deal with certain conceptual problems that Bion stresses and which are closely related to the practice of psychoanalysis.

When referring to the events of psychoanalytic experience, Bion uses the sign O to refer to psychic reality. As we have already pointed out (see chapter 4), O cannot be known, but can have "been." It can only reach the domain of K once it has been transformed through experience. Only then can it be formulated in terms of the sensuous elements of experience. Until that moment, its existence is a phenomenological conjecture.

Bion places a very special value on the formulations of those analytic events which take place during the course of the analysis, and which are different from those formulated outside the session. Their therapeutic value is even greater if they lead to transformations in O instead of transformations in K (see chapter 4). Thanks to the analysis he has to undergo during his analytic training, the analyst is better prepared to remove the obstacles he will find during his participation in the analytic experience. But other equipment of schemes, beliefs, and established conventions which may join with his patient's conscious or unconscious attacks on the analyst's capacity to think analytically can jeopardize the efficiency and freedom previously achieved by the analyst in his own analysis.

The analyst will try to direct his attention to O, the unknown and unknowable, while maintaining the psychoanalytic point of view or vertex. As soon as he can "be O," he will be in a position to know the events which are evolutions of O. The interpretation itself can constitute a true event in an evolution of O common to analyst and analysand alike. Both will depend not only on their respective sense but on the psychic qualities which can be perceived by intuition—as Freud pointed out—by that mental counterpart of the sense organs which he calls the "organ of consciousness."

It is impossible to establish rules for the moment in which the emotional experience is mature for interpretation, because there is an ineffable component in the analytic emotional experience. But it is possible to suggest rules, and

Bion tries to do so, to help the analyst achieve a mental state that will allow him to perceive the O of the analytic experience.

Bion suggests that the analyst should learn to work without "memory, desire, or understanding." Rather than *forgetting,* Bion postulates a positive act which restrains active memory and desire and provides a mental state which he represents by the term *faith.* It will allow him to approach the psychic reality that cannot be known but can "be been." It is a scientific "act of faith" quite different from the religious meaning ascribed it in conversational usage; it has an unconscious and unknown event in its background.

Bion uses the term *faith, act of faith,* and *mystery* in many of his papers to refer to a mental activity which operates in a non-sensuous dimension.

He proposes to examine what happens, for instance, with the phenomenon of anxiety. Nobody has any doubt about its existence or its reality. We are, nevertheless, referring to something which lacks a sensuous counterpart; it lacks form, color, smell; it is not accessible to the senses. To be truthful, our knowledge of anxiety depends on something different from sensuous experience. It is related rather to a capacity developed in analytic practice that allows us to detect, for example, that the patient hides his anxiety behind his hostile appearance.

This something which is different from sensuous experience and which is specifically important to the analyst's work, is *intuition.* It is based on an experience that does not have a sensuous background even though it can sometimes be expressed in terms derived from the language of the senses. One says, for example, "I see" to mean "I intuit."[2] Intuition consists in the specific capacity to perceive emotional states, and is part of the psychoanalytic function of the personality.[3] When, during the course of a psychoanalytic process, a growth of this function takes place in the analysand and the analyst, Bion suggests that an "evolution" of that analysis has taken place. For Bion, "evolution" can have a superficial similarity with memory, but once it has been experienced it is impossible to confuse the two. The term *memory* refers to that aspect of experience predominantly related to sensuous impressions. Memories are fragmented and must be actively sought out. On the other hand dreamlike memory or "evolution" can be compared with the substance of dreams and corresponds to psychic reality. It shares with the dreams "the quality of being totally present or inexplicably and suddenly absent." Evolution implies an ability to join, through sudden intuition, a series of incoherent and apparently unrelated phenomena that in this way acquire the coherence and meaning they were lacking.

The aim of a psychoanalytic treatment is mental growth. This is the psychoanalytic vertex from which Bion approaches the practice of psychoanalysis. Instead, the patient can approach psychoanalysis from different vertices: as an antidote against his psychotic anxieties, as a refuge from his psychopathology, to counteract his responsibilities vis-a-vis reality, as a search for advice and directions, for the solution of his daily difficulties, etc. Nevertheless, the patient comes to analysis with the wish to be "cured." Bion distinguishes between the vertex of the practice of psychoanalysis and the aim of "cure" as it is understood in medicine, with its associations of relieving pain, suppressing the illness, etc. Cure, with its sensuous background, as well as the "desire to cure and be cured," interferes with the capacity for evolution within the analysis.

Bion's suggestion about the advantage of dispensing with memory and desire can produce confusion and perplexity in the reader. It lends itself to misunderstandings which distort its true spirit. It proposes an internal attitude rather than a real modification of the analyst's technique with the patient. Bion particularly wishes to encourage that quality of functioning on the part of the analyst ("evolution") which will facilitate the full use of his intuition. It is in this sense that he suggests the advantages of "blinding oneself artificially" in order to work better. He bases this on a state described by Freud in one of his letters to Lou Andreas Salome,[4] which includes the following statement: "I know I have artificially blinded myself in my work, with the aim of concentrating all the light on the only dark passage." Bion means by this, that it is better for the analyst not to be influenced by his previous knowledge or his a priori judgment so as to avoid contaminating his evaluation of what is happening in the "here and now" of the analytic session. In this way, he can more fully grasp the new elements and shades that always exist in each separate encounter between analyst and patient. This implies giving up the conscious use of "memories" and "desires" that may or may not be linked with the patient, and rejecting the defensive use of his theoretical knowledge.

While the analyst (actively) tries to remember what the patient told him in the previous session (memory), or to think of what the patient will do at the end of the sessions, or of next weekend, or of his wish for the patient to improve and be "cured" (desire), he lessens the possibility of observing and perceiving the new facts which are evolving in the session at that moment.

Bion of course does not want to give the erroneous impression that he considers it would be good for the analyst to mutilate his personality in suppressing his memory and desire. He accepts that it is essential to preserve the capacity to remember events and past experiences and to have hopes and plans for the future. But he thinks the analyst can be sufficiently trained so as to retain his capacity to free himself temporarily of "memory" and "desire" whenever they appear as disturbing mental phenomena that threaten the profitable use of the analytic session. (See Appendix § 10.)

There is a general tendency to avoid new, incomprehensible, and incoherent situations because they produce anxiety and persecution. This happens not only in the patient but also in the analyst. For this reason, both of them unconsciously collude at times to deal only with things which are already known and thus easier to understand.

Bion advises the analyst to consider the patient "as if he were seen for the first time," a "new patient." This implies an ability to embark on the experience of each session with a free, unprejudiced mind so that observation is fully efficient and "evolution" or intuition can develop.

Notes

1. We shall include in this chapter some of the concepts on psychoanalytic technique developed by Bion in lectures to the Argentine Psychoanalytic Association during his stay in Buenos Aires in July 1968.

2. The metaphorical sense of "I see" does not exist when the psychotic patient uses this phrase. Instead of "I see" meaning "I understand," it may mean that the interpretation has been perceived by the patient in a visual or hallucinatory form, and that it has not been understood.

3. The term *reverie* refers to an import function of the mother in her emotional contact with the baby and refers mainly to non-sensuous elements; this funciton can be extended to describe the analyst who is in receipt of the projective identifications of his patient and proceeds to make contact through his intuition with the sensuous elements of the patient's psychic reality.

4. Sigmund Freud and Lou Andreas Salome, *Correspondence,* compiled by Ernst Pfeiffer.

Appendix:
Notes to the Second Edition

1. A question we do not discuss in the first edition is developed by Bion in his *Experiencias en grupo* (Group experiences, Paidos, Buenos Aires, second edition, 1972) as the concept of protomental system.

Bion indicates that the psychological structure of a complex group, or work group (wg) is very powerful: being a very lively structure, the individuals in the group are disproportionately afraid of being suffocated or invaded by the emotional states of the basic assumption. To these fears must be added the fear provoked by the lack of knowledge of the forces opposing the group.

If, in a given group, the forces in conflict can be characterized as, for example, work group (wg) as opposed to the basic assumption of dependency (baD), we may wonder about the fate of the basic assumption of pairing (baP) and of the basic assumption of fight-flight (baF). We can also relate this question to another: what causes the emotions linked to the basic assumption to remain so tenaciously linked to one another?

In order to answer these two questions (the fate of nonoperational basic assumptions and the tenacity of the emotions belonging to the basic assumption), Bion postulates the existence of "protomental" phenomena.

This concept transcends experience but Bion believes that it is necessary in order to articulate his ideas.

The protomental state or activity can be characterized as neither psychic nor physical; its evolution, rather, produces psychic or physical phenomena. It is a system in which those aspects remain undifferentiated; it is a matrix from which phenomena appear.

From this matrix (protomental system) stem the basic emotions belonging to a basic assumption that, at a given moment, tenaciously dominates the mental life of the group. The nonoperational basic assumptions remain, so to speak, within the limits of the protomental system.

Those protomental levels are the origins of the illnesses of the group.

In short, the illnesses of the group must be sought in: (1) the relation of the individual to a particular basic assumption, both in case he tries to maintain it or in case he fights against it, and (2) in the protomental stages of other nonoperational basic assumptions at a given moment.

The concept of protomental system and the theories of basic assumptions can be utilized in order to provide a new perspective in relation to psychic illnesses. We should remember that protomental systems (pmD, pmF, pmP) constitute a basis or matrix for the groups which, in the course of evolution, will appear either as psychic phenomena linked with the active basic assumption or as physical phenomena. The classification of physical illnesses—also called psychosomatic illnesses—according to their origin in a given protomental system linking them with the associated emotional structure implies opening a perspective for research in the field of psychosomatic medicine which surpasses current psychosomatic notions and lends to the physical illness a group dimension not yet explored.

Furthermore, the field of application of the notion of protomental system can be extended speculatively to the realm of money and its use. Bion thinks that the value of money has not only a commercial origin in the value of goods and the need for exchange, but has also a group origin, linked to a given basic assumption, in the evolution of the protomental system.

According to him, the origin of currency would lie not in the necessity for exchange but, on the contrary, in the need of a value accepted by the group in its entirety, as, for example, the "price for the bride"; currency would also have been a means of compensating a group for the loss of one of its members.

His intention is not to subordinate the use of currency or its fluctuations to any one concrete basic assumption, although it would be possible to detect particular types of relationships, since money does not have the same meaning in a warfare group or society, under the fight-flight basic assumption, that it has in a religious society. If the notions belonging to the protomental system can be used to understand physical and psychic illnesses, these, too, can be considered, within economic science, as illnesses of the exchange mechanism.

The fluctuations in the value of currency would undeniably be linked with the active basic assumption and would depend on the protomental system.

2. As Bion sees it, the projective identification has been formulated in terms derived from a realization of the idea of an individual's three dimensional space. According to this Kleinian formulation there would be some objects in that space into which the patients supposedly project previously

dissociated parts of their own personality. The degree of fragmentation and the distance to which the fragments have been projected would be the main factors in determining the degree of mental disturbance displayed by the patient in his contact with reality. Bion's experience with most disturbed patients has convinced him of the need for a new hypothesis that would provide a deeper understanding of their behavior and reactions. The case in point concerns those personalities with a strong intolerance for frustration and psychic pain; they feel the pain but cannot "suffer" it. The patient who cannot stand his pain also fails to experience or "suffer" pleasure. He loses the ability to symbolize and abstract, words for him becoming indistinguishable from things-in-themselves; they cease being representations and become concrete elements or beta elements.

These regressive patients therefore lack the equipment that would help them to "map" the realization of a mental space and to form an adequate notion of the existence of external space. Less regressive patients would make use of projective identification in order to situate the fragmented aspects of the self onto external objects, but the more regressive ones would feel incapable of projecting the divided parts of their personalities since they lack the notion of containers into which the projection might take place. On the other hand, they would form the notion of "explosive projective identification" in a vast space, a rather limitless space which cannot be represented in any way whatsoever. They live through their emotions as if these were thrown across and got lost in the immensity. What to the observer should appear as thoughts, visual images, and verbalizations is seen by the patient as language shreds and disperse emotional experiences, within a space lacking time and space boundaries. This generates a very intense fear, a psychotic panic, or a psychotic catastrophe.

Bion differentiates between projective identification and another group of realizations acquiring a configuration called by him *hyperbole*. This term corresponds to the observation theories system and represents a series of clinical statements revealing projection, rivalry, ambition, violence, and the distance to which an object or an aspect of an object has been projected. By way of example, we present two remarks by a patient reported by Bion: (1) "I always thought that you were a good analyst"; (2) "When I was a child, I met a woman in Peru who was a seer." We can see how the analyst's "goodness," through rivalry, has been projected toward a distant time and place.

In another type of patient, the psychotic personality offers similar characteristics in relation to intolerance for frustration. But it differentiates itself from the first type through the utilization of a splitting mechanism different from the one just described; this mechanism consists in the formation of "bizarre" objects. Here the dissociation process has a more passive bias, giving way to what Meltzer has termed *dismantling* of the personality, which is reduced to its primitive perceptual abilities. The patient is reduced to a state of mindlessness, a lack of mind characteristic of the autistic personality, and has difficulties discriminating between animate and inanimate objects, etc. (D. Meltzer, J. Bremner, Sh. Hoxter, D. Weddell, I. Wittenberg, *Explorations in Autism*, Clunie Press, London, 1975).

Due to the lack of a maternal object, which would adequately function as a means of limiting evacuations and projections, there has not been for these patients a possibility of apprehending the notion either of the self's internal space or of its objects. At a certain point, they were incapable of distinguishing between being inside or outside the objects; therefore, they had serious difficulties when using the projection and introjection mechanisms. In the same way, they were incapable of using projective identification as a device functioning in a world understood as three-dimensional. This is the reason why these patients apparently use a specific mechanism of narcissistic identification, called "adhesive identification" by E. Bick ("The experience of the skin in early object relations," *International Journal of Psycho-Analysis* 49, 1968). This type of identification can produce an extreme dependence on objects, stimulating the fantasy of their being stuck like a postage stamp to the surface of the object so that they become a part of that object, imitating its appearance and behavior.

The history of Palinurus' death, as described in Virgil's *Aeneid* (which will be referred to in the notes to chapter 6) provides a model for the representation of a psychotic part of the personality.

3. A danger connected with the use of models is that they tend to suppress in the analyst the ability to observe. Observation is basic and essential in order to develop the psychoanalytic function of personality. If the model is substituted for observation, comprehension becomes obstructed and the investigation of related elements impossible.

4. In an unpublished paper ("The grid"), written in Los Angeles in 1971, Bion points out that row C as well as column 2 deserve to be extended even to the point of forming a separate grid.

Column 2 Bion originally conceived to provide a series of categories for statements known by both patient and analyst to be false. An example might be, "I will wait for you tomorrow at dawn." In clinical practice, however, it became necessary to consider the special problems created by lying. It is useful to distinguish between false statements and lying statements. False formulations are related to the inadequacies of human beings, who cannot entirely trust their ability to realize "truth" and formulate it adequately. On the other hand, the lying personality needs to be sure of its knowledge of the truth, and its statements, emphatically "true" but really lying, serve the purpose of avoiding a certain knowledge; therefore, column 2 should include a column 2' for the lying statements. These are characterized by their substitution for "true" statements which would otherwise provoke catastrophic change.

Row C also deserves a separate grid.

This row includes images, primarily visual, such as they appear in dreams, myths, verbal accounts of visual images, and hallucinations.

The complexity of row C justifies its extension to include transformations of sense experience other than the visual. The grid can also be extended in other ways. If, for example, the analyst wishes to investigate the distance between physical and psychic facts, he can introduce, between rows A and B, the whole grid, as if inside the grid one could see many grids in depth. He could in this way extend the grid indefinitely, provided he gave an explanation of this operation as constituting a second cycle. Bion says that he can visualize the grid as repeating itself in a helicoidal way.

5. Geometry made progress through the discovery of Cartesian coordinates, mathematics through the inclusion first of negative and then of imaginary numbers. Psychoanalysis has a similar need for formulations advancing our understanding of the mind.

Bion gives as an example three cases of a straight line in relation to a circle: (1) points real and different (secant line), (2) points real and coincident (when the straight line cuts the circle at a single point—tangent line), and (3) conjugated ensemble (when the line is completely out of the circle). The circle is a useful image for many individuals, since it can illustrate visually the "inside and outside"; for the psychotic personality, though, it is an evidence of the nonexistence of a dividing membrane. The psychotic personality cannot tolerate the non-thing, and sees the circle as a reminder of a non-thing that hinders its discrimination between "an inside and an outside."

From another perspective, we could apply this mathematical model to several situations belonging to psychoanalytical theory and clinical practice. The first case, the circle cut by the straight line in two points (secant) may represent the discrimination between subject and object, inside and outside, reality and fantasy, symbol and symbolized, etc. The second case, the circle touched by the straight line in one point (tangent) may represent, for example, the state of confusion between internal and external world, etc. The third case, the circle and the line totally separated, without a single point of contact (conjugated ensemble) may represent the "psychotic personality" without contact with reality, or the psychotic personality as separated from neurotic personality, or the lack of contact between patient and analyst, etc.

6. Myths (on the grid, formulations in row C) are used by Bion to form a "picture gallery" of verbal elements which can serve as a model for almost any aspect related to emotional situations belonging to the field of intersection between practical psychoanalysis and psychoanalytic theory. To the well-known Oedipus, Tower of Babel, and Garden of Eden myths he has added at least two "new pictures": the real cemetery of Ur and the death of Palinurus.

Approximately 3500 years before Christ, a king was buried in the real cemetery of Ur. According to the reconstruction made by the expedition from the British Museum and Pennsylvania University under Sir Leonard Wooley, the burial ceremony included a procession formed by the most distinguished dignitaries of the court, who, dressed in all splendor, descended into a hole especially prepared and there took a narcotic potion (probably hashish). Then, with musical accompaniment, the hole was filled with earth and its occupants buried alive together with the deceased monarch.

Bion wonders what forces—emotional, cultural, religious—led the members of that court to a behavior that surely caused their death. He wonders also whether there is an equivalent force today, without our realizing the danger. What force are we talking about? Can we call it "ignorance"? Or should we think that it is a more dynamic force, a less known one? Is it "religion"? Or is it "omnipotence"?

To this "picture" Bion adds another: the tomb robbers, who, violating a field sanctified by rituals and magic, five hundred years later ransacked the same cemetery. He wonders again what emotional forces drove those men to penetrate a place still charged with magic, overcoming their fear of meeting the spirits of the dead and the anger of the gods. The robbers, by defying fear, found the royal tomb, and took many of the buried objects. Was it curiosity, the force that led them to do so? Or greed perhaps? Bion suggests that we should consider those robbers as pioneer scientists . . . or condemn our scientists for their greed.

The two pictures suggest many analogies and can be used—together with the period of time that separates them—to build a model which would enrich the perspective of situations or conflicts faced by the psychoanalyst in his practice.

Another picture, this one from Virgil's *Aeneid*, is Palinurus' death (*Aeneid*, Book V), the details of which we transcribe: Aeneas has been reassured by Neptune after a storm, and orders his fleet to take advantage of the calm weather in order to continue the journey. He puts the fleet under the command of Palinurus. While everyone is asleep, Palinurus takes the helm and follows the stars. Somnus sends Palinurus grim visions. Disguised as Phorbas, Somnus sits by Palinurus and talks to him: "Palinurus, son of Iasio, see how the waves by themselves lead the fleet; the winds blow softly; this is a time for rest; put your head and eyes to rest. I will replace you for a while." Raising his tired eyes, Palinurus answers: "Do you want me to ignore what a calm sea and peaceful waves really are? Do you want me to trust this monster? Do you want me to entrust Aeneas' fate to untrustworthy winds which have deceived me so many times under the guise of a serene sky?" On saying this, he gathers all his strength and rises, and neither leaves the helm for a moment nor ceases to watch the stars; but the god throws over his temples Lethean forgetfulness; an invincible torpor invades him and in spite of his efforts his eyes are invaded by sleep. No sooner does the lethargy begin to invade Palinurus' limbs, than the god leans over him and throws him into the waves; Palinurus, in his fall, carries with him a part of the stern and the helm; he calls his companions repeatedly but in vain.

In the meantime, the fleet pursues its way through the sea as if nothing had happened, trusting to the promises of Father Neptune.

Aeneas becomes aware that his ship, having lost Palinurus, is wandering haphazardly through the sea, and he himself takes the lead in the midst of darkness, and saddened, bewailing his lost friend, says: "Oh Palinurus, by your excessive trust in the calm of sky and sea, you are going to lie unburied over the anonymous sand."

This striking story is full of suggestions. It is striking in its narrative and pictorial qualities, and by virtue of its language also, which, as in Sophocles' *Oedipus Rex*, lends dramatic form to the constant conjunction expressed by the myth. Here we find, as in the cemetery of Ur, emotional forces, gods, drugs, violence and arrogance, omnipotence, and hopelessness.

The psychoanalyst, sheltered in the apparent calm of his offices, faces the evolution of the most primitive parts of the mind, the real and omnipotent process of pathologic projective identification, the attack on the therapeutic bond, or psychosis. As a tomb robber, the psychoanalyst is afraid of the consequences of his attempt to delve in such dangerous fields; like Palinurus, he runs the risk of failing in his attempt and being condemned for his irresponsibility.

These are some of the possible uses of the "pictures" offered by Bion. Each reader can find in them the meanings suggested by his own experience.

7. The "point of view" implies vision. It is possible, however, to think of other senses as the vertex from which transformations are developed. When a line is visualized without representing it on paper, one does something that has been described as "using the internal eye," "seeing with the imagination," or "visualizing." This activity depends on the mental counterpart of the visual sense. Similarly, the "bitterness" of a memory depends on the mental counterpart of the nourishment system; the "bad smell" of a situation, on the mental counterpart of the olfactory sense. In this way, and by comparison with the internal eye, it is possible to speak of an olfactory vertex, or of an auditive, breathing, reproductive vertex, etc.

In any case, the visual-mental counterpart seems to have the upper hand over all the other mental counterparts, due to the fact that visual images can better adapt to other media, to the verbal, for example. For this reason Bion thinks that a possible solution to the problem of psychoanalytic communication can be found, for the time being, through the elements of row C.

8. *Transference* is an analytic term implying a relationship between two elements. If, for example, between analyst and patient the roles of father and son are reflected, what is important is not the signification of each of these roles separately but their relationship. What is called by the analyst transference is similar to what mathematicians call pure mathematics, which refers to the relationship between two mathematical objects.

9. The term *science*, in its usual sense, describes a certain activity toward the objects of the senses; it is not adequate to describe an approach to the realities of the psychoanalytical "science." The latter occupies itself with that aspect of human personality which is, ultimately, unknown and unknowable—O. This criticism is valid regardless of which of the vertices is involved: all of them (with the possible exception of the mystic-religious) are inadequate in regard to O, since they do not adapt to what lacks a basis in the senses.

10. Analysis is done in the present. It cannot be otherwise. Even if the analyst or the patient refers to ideas related to the past (nostalgias) or to the future (anticipations), these ideas imply present feelings.

We should have in mind Bion's notion that there should be, in the analyst's office, two people who share in the anxiety-generating situation, even if the anguish is different for each. When this does not happen, one might well ask why they bother to learn what everyone knows. This would imply working only on what is already known—a very strong temptation for analysts, since analysis creates a situation in which ordinary human beings devote themselves to a very anguishing occupation without even leaving their homes.

The analyst must be able to tolerate the expanding universe that appears in front of him through his relationship with the patient. He could, he thinks, pass from nothingness to interpretation, but by the time he has finished talking the universe has expanded beyond his own perception. The problem is how to stand all this, a much humbler objective than trying to add something new to psychoanalysis.

The practice of psychoanalysis depends on the analyst's and the patient's ability to establish contact with the psychoanalytic fact. To speak of psychoanalytic facts is in itself to theorize, so that an appreciation or clear comprehension of the psychoanalytic facts is required. In the analyst's office his practice provides him with opportunities to say: "This is what I call a fact."

Bion uses a model in order to illustrate certain kinds of experience within the psychoanalytic situation. He says that if he looked at a current of water flowing calmly for lack of obstacles, he would not be able to see it, since it would be too transparent; but if he introduced a stick in the water, he could see the current in the turbulence thus provoked. In the same way, he points out, if we supposed the existence of a human mind, that mind would be capable, at one moment or another, of generating some turbulence; other human minds would be capable, through their sensibility, intuition, or talent, to make that turbulence manifest; such is the case of Leonardo da Vinci.

Bion says that the tension between two people can be so low that they do not stimulate each other. On the other hand, the differences between attitudes or temperament can be so great that discussion becomes impossible. The situation could be so lacking in tension that there would be no stimulus, or so tense that it would not be productive.

Glossary of Signs

baD Basic assumption of dependency: represents a group mentality characterized by the collective fantasy of depending on a leader for their mental and physical nourishment.

baF Basic assumption of fight-flight: represents a group mentality that contains the collective fantasy of attacking and being attacked.

baP Basic assumption of pairing: represents a group mentality dominated by the messianic hope of a leader who is to be born.

W Work group: is the mental activity of a group which has the characteristic of carrying out its tasks by rational and scientific methods.

♀♂ Represents the dynamic interaction between the container and the contained. It symbolizes the mechanism of projective identification and is also an element of psychoanalysis.

Ps ↔ D Represents the interaction between the paranoid-schizoid position and the depressive position, as well as the emergence of the selected fact.

R Symbolizes reason.

I Symbolizes ideas, and all that can be included under the heading of "thought."

± Y ( ) ( ) ( ) Represents the psychoanalytic object.

μ (mu) Represents the innate character of the personality.

ξ (epsilon) Represents the non-saturated element that is present in the preconception and open to the approaching realization.

ψ (psi) Represents the preconception.

Y Represents a factor of mental growth.

L Represents the link of love between two people or two parts of the same person.

H Represents the link of hate between two people or between two parts of the same person.

K Represents the link of knowledge.

–K Represents the ♀ and ♂ as linked by not-knowing; it does not mean the absence of knowledge but an active situation where the relationship is deprived of meaning.

T Represents a transformation which

	includes the original event, the process, and the end-product.
T α	Represents the process of transformation.
T β	Represents the end-product of a transformation.
T (patient) α	Represents the process of transformation in the patient.
T (patient) β	Represents the end-product of a transformation in the patient.
T (analyst) α	Represents the process of transformation in the analyst.
T (analyst) β	Represents the end-product of a transformation in the analyst.
. and —	(point and line) Represents among other things, the time and the space that can themselves symbolize objects and object relations. The point (.) and the line (—) express "the position the object occupies in space and time" as a more elaborate response of the non-psychotic part of the personality when confronted with the absence of the object.
O	(the letter "O") Represents ultimate reality, absolute truth, or unknowable psychic reality in the Kantian sense, which can only be known through its transformations.
F	(act of faith) Represents a mental attitude favored by "no-memory," "no-desire," "no-understanding," destined to perceive the evolutions of O.
–F	Represents a greedy, envious force destined to strip the objects of their existence.

Chronological List
of Bion's Writings

1948   Psychiatry at a time of crisis. *British Journal of Medical Psychology* 21:81ff.

1950   The imaginary twin. Read to the British Psychoanalytic Society in 1950. In *Second Thoughts*, London: Heinemann, 1967.

1952   Group dynamics: a review. *International Journal of Psycho-Analysis* 33:235 ff. In *New Directions in Psycho-Analysis*, London: Tavistock, 1953.

1954   Notes on the theory of schizophrenia. *International Journal of Psycho-Analysis* 35:113ff. In *Second Thoughts*, 1967.

1955   Language and the schizophrenic. In *New Directions in Psycho-Analysis*, London: Tavistock, 1955.

1956   Development of schizophrenic thought. *International Journal of Psycho-Analysis* 37:344ff. In *Second Thoughts*, 1967.

1957   Differentiation of the psychotic from the non-psychotic personalities. *International Journal of Psycho-Analysis* 38:266ff. In *Second Thoughts,* 1967.

1958   On arrogance. *International Journal of Psycho-Analysis* 39:144ff. In *Second Thoughts,* 1967.

1958   On hallucination. *International Journal of Psycho-Analysis* 39:341ff. In *Second Thoughts,* 1967.

1959   Attacks on linking. *International Journal of Psycho-Analysis* 40:308ff. In *Second Thoughts,* 1967.

1959   *Experiences in Groups.* London: Tavistock.

1962   A theory of thinking. *International Journal of Psycho-Analysis* 43:306ff.

1962   *Learning from Experience.* London: Heinemann.

1963   *Elements of Psycho-Analysis.* London: Heinemann.

1965   *Transformations.* London: Heinemann.

1966   Catastrophic change. Unpublished, transcribed in the *Scientific Bulletin of the British Psychoanalytical Society* 5.

1967   Notes on memory and desire. *Psychoanalytic Forum* II, 3.

1967   *Second Thoughts.* London: Heinemann.

1970   *Attention and Interpretation.* London: Tavistock.

1975   A Memoir of the Future—To be published.
          Guilt for Crimes Already Forgiven. In preparation.

1977   *Seven Servants: Four Works by Wilfred R. Bion* (collects *Learning from Experience, Elements of Psycho-Analysis, Transformations,* and *Attention and Interpretation*). New York: Jason Aronson.